La Finca

Love, Loss,
and Laundry
on a Tiny
Puerto Rican
Island

La Finca

A love story and memory
of a finca,
Puerto Rican island

Corky Parker

La Finca

Love, Loss, and Laundry on a Tiny Puerto Rican Island

Corky Parker

Trinity University Press
San Antonio

Published by Trinity University Press
San Antonio, Texas 78212

Book design by Corky Parker and Pinafore Press / Janice Shay
Cover design by Kevin Cox
"The Guest House," by Rumi. English translation copyright © 2004
    Coleman Barks. Reprinted by permission of Coleman Barks.
"La Finca Pasta" recipe, by Alice Waters. Copyright © 2013 Alice Waters.
    Reprinted by permission of Alice Waters.

ISBN 978-1-59534-905-7 hardcover
ISBN 978-1-59534-906-4 ebook

Trinity University Press strives to produce its books using methods
and materials in an environmentally sensitive manner. We favor working
with manufacturers that practice sustainable management of all natural
resources, produce paper using recycled stock, and manage forests with
the best possible practices for people, biodiversity, and sustainability. The
press is a member of the Green Press Initiative, a nonprofit program dedicated to supporting publishers in their efforts to reduce their impacts on
endangered forests, climate change, and forest-dependent communities.

The paper used in this publication meets the minimum requirements of
the American National Standard for Information Sciences–Permanence of
Paper for Printed Library Materials, ANSI 39.48–1992.

CIP data on file at the Library of Congress

25 24 23 22 21 | 5 4 3 2 1

Printed in Canada

For
Tyler, Gus, & Xing Ji
David, Anne, & Bill
and all whose hearts are moved
by the old blue house with the big yellow sun,
Casa Grande

"the sense of standing on a threshold, while your old still remained knowable and holdable and not yet lost"

—Richard Flanagan

Contents

Property Map 8–9

Guide to Key Characters 10–11

Introduction 13

1. Living the Dream 17

2. Hatching the Plan 25

3. Exploring the New World 31

4. Finding New Dawn 41

5. On Our Own 51

6. A Month of Firsts 57

7. At the Helm 69

8. Happy Traveling 75

9. The Losing End 79

10. Solo 87

11. Aftermath 95

12. Meanwhile, Back at La Finca 103

13. On-the-Job Life Lessons 107

14. Bill 117

15. Chaos of Construction 125

16. Another Day in Paradise 133

17. No Stopping This Carnival 143

18. Smooth Sailing 153

19. When Alice Comes to Visit 165

20. Being Here Now, Finally 177

21. The Winter Things Couldn't Get Right .. 185

22. How and ¿Por qué? 195

Epilogue 199

Acknowledgments 207

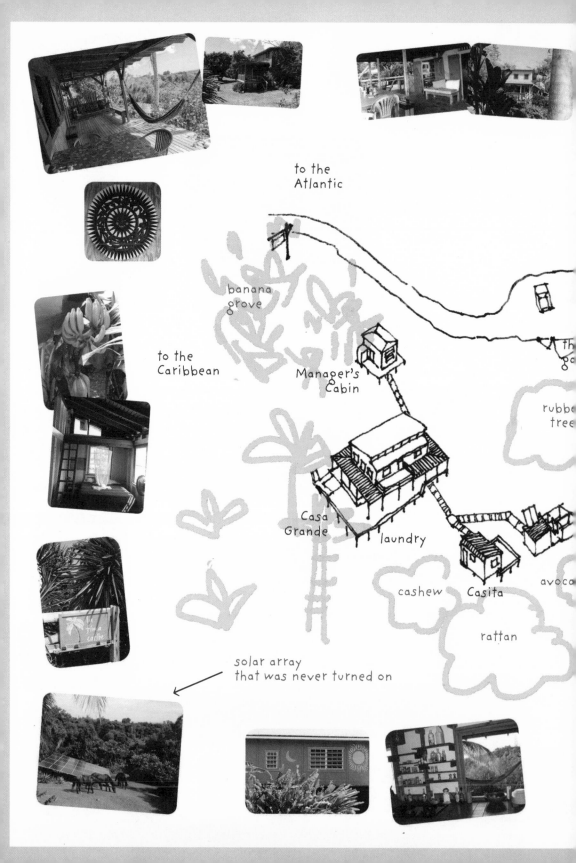

to the
Atlantic

banana
grove

to the
Caribbean

Manager's
Cabin

rubber
tree

th
ga

Casa
Grande

laundry

Casita

cashew

avoca

rattan

solar array
that was never turned on

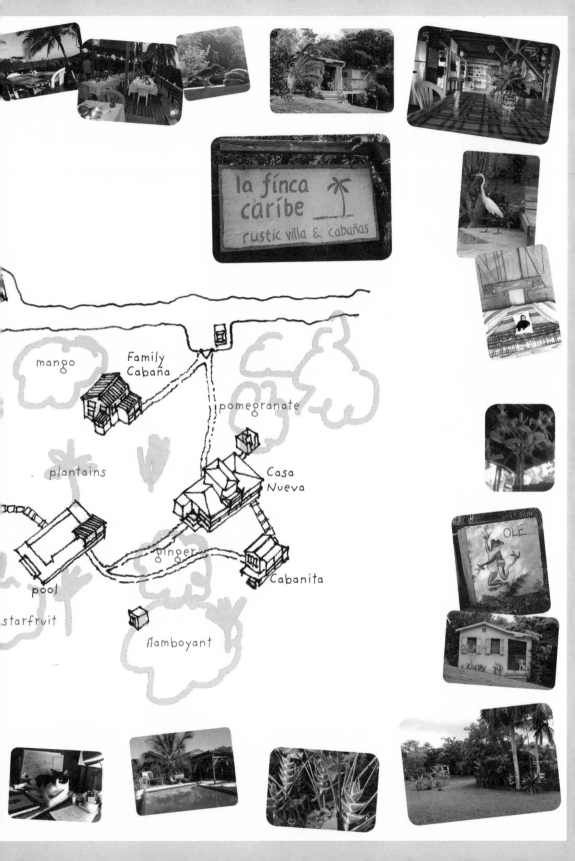

la finca caribe

rustic villa & cabañas

mango

Family Cabaña

pomegranate

plantains

Casa Nueva

ginger

Cabanita

pool

starfruit

flamboyant

OLÉ

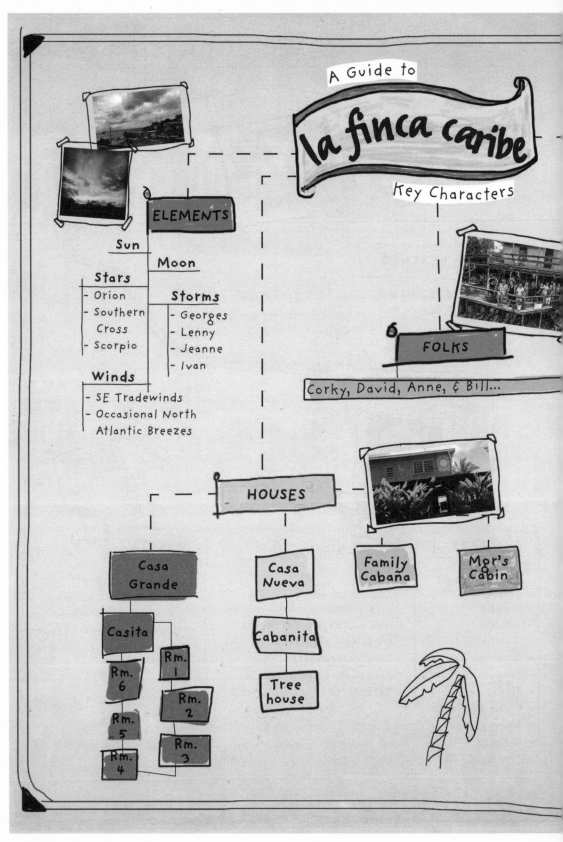

A Guide to

la finca caribe

Key Characters

ELEMENTS

Sun

Moon

Stars
- Orion
- Southern Cross
- Scorpio

Storms
- Georges
- Lenny
- Jeanne
- Ivan

Winds
- SE Tradewinds
- Occasional North Atlantic Breezes

FOLKS

Corky, David, Anne, & Bill...

HOUSES

Casa Grande

Casa Nueva

Family Cabaña

Mor's Cabin

Casita

Cabanita

Rm. 6

Rm. 1

Rm. 5

Rm. 2

Rm. 4

Rm. 3

Tree house

scalawags...

...and the long line of caretakers and

...wit, Scott, Bill T, Wendy, Derrick, Pam, Graham,

BEACHES

- Blue/Chivas
- Plata
- Garcia

- Navio
- Corcho
- Media Luna

- Green
- Sun
- Gringo

CRITTERS

Cats & Dogs

- Phoebe
- Samson
- Mambo
- Sunshine
- Ziggy
- Blanca
- Tiene Leche
- Smidge
- Botones
- The White Cat

Misc.

- Lisa Simpson, Iguana
- Navio & Verde, Parakeets
- Lil Buddy, Sink frog
- Tree caterpillars
- Flamboyant Mockingbird
- Tarantulas

GUESTS

- writing workshop
- secret celebrities
- the new Scandinavians
- hard-working work traders
- friends & family
- just folks
- family reunions
- romantic interludes
- urban hipsters
- yoga retreats
- covens

This is a story about La Finca Caribe, three acres in the hills of Vieques, a small island in the Caribbean.

Introduction

Guests ask. All the time. "So what made you want to do this?" "How'd you . . . ?" or "Why . . . ?"

Funny, it seems so natural to me. Don't we all want to grow up to be inn-keepers on tiny tropical islands? Isn't the *Swept Away/Gilligan's Island/Fawlty Towers* combo fantasy simply basic human nature? Regardless, I never know how serious the guests are, or how much time they have. Because answering could take a while.

Sometimes I wonder if they're asking for do-it-yourself instructions on how to ditch the work world. They may want to know if it's safe, or a good investment, or if anyone can do it. Sometimes they're pretty open about being jealous of my good luck—I've learned to laugh that one off. I'm usually busy hanging the laundry, or duct-taping a fix to some emergency, so I am able to dodge the questions. But even if I am in the mood and have the time to answer, I still get stymied on where to begin. It's a bit like peeling an onion. One layer reveals more of what's underneath. If I go deep enough, someone might end up crying.

Truth is, I'm not sure exactly what made me fall in love with a piece of property on a small Puerto Rican island when I was forty years old, now twenty years ago. Not just fall in love, mind you, but act on it—make a commitment, and to a foreigner no less.

This is the story of La Finca Caribe: three acres in the hills of Vieques, a small Caribbean island just off Puerto Rico's eastern coast. It's about why and how I and my family found it, loved it, and held onto it—even though we had pretty much no idea what we were doing. It's about listening—even in the din of tropical depressions—to your spirit place, inside and out. Ultimately, it's about discovering how much we can learn from a place, and the futility of asking, ¿*Por qué?*

It's difficult, and a little daunting to try and capture one's memories over forty years with certitude. I'm so bad with numbers, whole years could be off. Luckily, I usually have my journal and sketchbook nearby as some oddball form of witness. Nonetheless, in case I got anything wrong, I've changed some names and locations, and condensed conversations to the best of my memory. The part about the magic, though—I'm totally clear about that.

There's a goat leg in the front yard,

a small frog who lives in my shower,

a bong on the front desk,

and a guest's underwear soaking in the main house kitchen sink.

BEWARE....
of the NAYSAYERS!

who say

YOU CAN'T...

ask guests to use the same two towels for a week

KEEP GROWING GARLIC OUT OF YOUR SINK DRAIN

run an inn from 4,000 miles away

not take credit cards

let your kids fly home without you

DO IT ON YOUR OWN

SHOW YOUR FRAYED EDGES

be serious about

wearing that muumuu

cook dinner for Alice Waters

Oh, and you can't write a book in varying tenses, with this whole journal thing you have going on

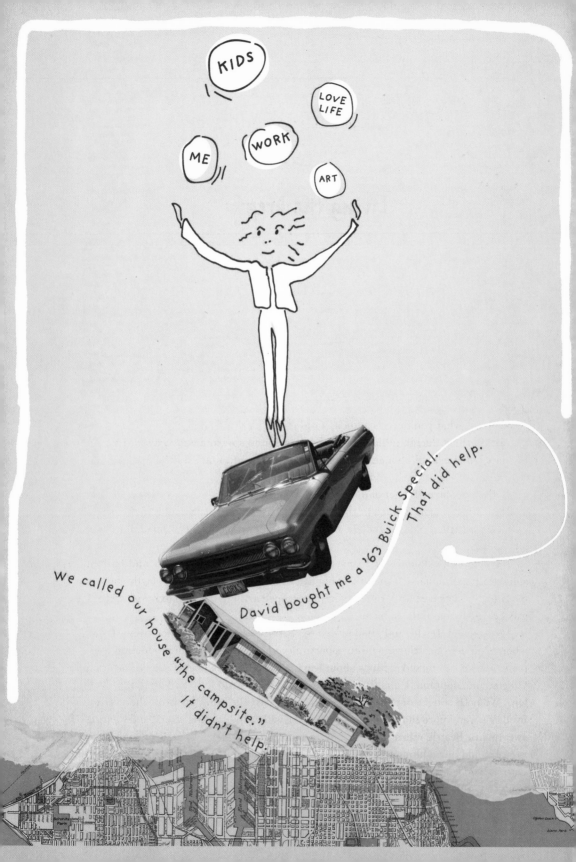

1.

Living the Dream

"Corcho, what you need is a finca."

Rocio's thick Barranquillan accent made it sound so exotic: a *feeeenka*. I was in my early thirties, old enough to have traveled a bit, and knew a little Spanish, but not this.

"Okay . . . Maybe I'll get one, Rocio . . . What's a finca?"

"Finca just means a place in the country, like a ranch, a farm, a beach house, or just a little garden plot, anywhere you go to escape from the city. You're not a city girl, Corcho."

I wonder what Rocio saw in me at the time—young wife, mother, and harried small business manager—that made her see so clearly what I needed. Maybe she was psychic. She was certainly right about the escape part. I had begun to wonder what I was I doing living in the suburbs.

My husband, David, and I had moved to Seattle with our baby, Tyler, from Alaska, where we'd met. Seattle held more opportunity for growing our film production company, but we had mixed feelings about leaving Alaska's open beauty. David was from Oregon and Montana. I was from northern California, and lived in Vermont for college. We both sought out the far horizon, or at least the rural parts of wherever we lived. We were more than comfortable heating with wood, rafting rivers, and wearing sweatpants. Seattle was a rugged, soon-to-be-grungy city back then. It seemed natural we would buy a home to the north, far enough out of town to have a woodsy yard with raccoons and possums. It helped us feel at least distantly related to our wild, wilderness-filled pasts. It was 1986. Tyler was in preschool.

One rarely just drifts to
an island by accident,
like you might slide
to the next town, or
the wrong side of the
tracks.

Islands require some
kind of conscious
thought.

A move to an island is
deliberate and often
involves some notion
of escaping the rest of
the world.

I've lived on three.

I had wanted to get "a real job" in Seattle for a few years and then bring all the business savvy I could soak up back to our mom-and-pop creative team. The winery where I had been hired to manage public relations and write wine labels (and ignore the executive's overt flirtations) seemed as unreal as its phony "French chateau" headquarters. My female coworkers seemed hell-bent on climbing the corporate ladder in those godforsaken padded-shoulder suits and girl-style neckties that only served to strangle me.

Even in our midthirties, David and I wanted to escape our own emerging rat race. We were equal parts grossed out and bored by what seemed to be a new and growing American Dream, something called a lifestyle: yuppie-ness. It had its own handbook that listed the attributes—a whole host of perils and comforts that scared us. I can see now that we were probably afraid of losing our wild edge, nervous that cushy living would soften us. My corporate stint had to be brief. No wonder Rocio's advice felt so right.

The week our second son, Gus, was born, I quit the winery and went back to work with David at Merwin Creative. My three years in the corporate world had been a perfect training ground for pitching our services. Some of my coworkers were leaving the winery to work at a new business venture down the road, Microsoft. No one could really explain to me what this company did, or what software was, so I stuck with the plan of working with David. Besides, maybe our friends heading to Microsoft would hire us if the company needed film and creative services.

The search for a finca took some time. It began with us looking for a little weekend place. We'd visit friends in their various getaways—on farms or cabins in the mountains, islands, and waterways of Puget Sound. As sweet as they all looked, the notion of owning and caring for two lawnmowers and barbeques and schlepping away every weekend was less appealing. We refocused our search on an escape that was nearer to town. someplace rural enough to feel right but where we could still get in and out of the city for work. On weekends we'd bundle up the kids and go looking.

Vashon Island, a ferry away from downtown Seattle, looked just the part. It was late spring; the whole island was a little shaggy, the grass long and wet. On our first day looking for a house, we could easily have missed it—we weren't even to the top of the long first hill when we spotted the sign: *Farmhouse with pool.* OPEN HOUSE.

"It's an omen," David says. "You know how I've always wanted a pool."

"Yep, and I've always known you were crazy. We don't have the money for a pool, David. But what the heck, it says farmhouse, too. Let's go check it out. The boys want out of the car."

The big red house was on a hill looking north over Puget Sound, all the way to Canada—a house that seemed a dream come true for all of us, in different ways. For me, it was the two acres with fruit trees; for the boys, it was the forests that rimmed the land; and for David, it was that funky thirty-year-old saltwater pool.

"I think having a pool would probably be the coolest thing in the entire universe," Ty said to Gus. "Cool all the way to the moon and the stars. Right?" Ty was supporting his dad's platform and seeing very accurately into his own future.

"Yeah, Ty. I do too." Gus always sounded emphatic. He was in Ty's camp, of course, forever the little brother and first mate. "Right, Mommy?" He circled back to me.

I can imagine his three-year-old mind working: *A house with a pool is too good to be true: Mommy better be okay with it.* I was.

For the next twelve years, life on Vashon was a frenetic juggling act of child-rearing, housekeeping, growing a new business, nursing typical childhood ailments, and marriage counseling. I drove way too fast between client pitches, ferries, and soccer matches, and was always just a little late for everything. And then there was our weekly date night, dinner and the movies: a surefire way to keep the love alive, right?

It turns out Vashon wasn't an escape from the rat race.

In May 1995, David and I adopted our third child, a daughter, Xing Ji. I had always wanted a large family, so with Xing's arrival the family was complete. She was almost four years old, Tyler was eleven, and Gus was seven. The three kids tipped the scales—now they outnumbered us.

Ty was passionate about all things baseball. At that time the Seattle Mariners were on a major roll, and Ken Griffey Jr. was the superstar. Ty had decided that he wanted to bring his new little sister a baseball cap when we went to get her in China. "Yep. A Mariners cap. It's something she's going to need when she gets here. Especially if they make the World Series." I loved his planning. He was so confident. And he was right. She wore that hat from day one. She saw how proud it made him.

Meanwhile, Gus had been studying China in Mrs. Marr's first-grade class. Perfect timing. "I'm gonna bring her a set of markers, Mom. We found out the kids in China don't have them." Gus was right about his gift too. Xing kept those markers handy in the little backpack we brought her, ready to draw everything and anything. Like on her own arm the day we were kept waiting in Chengdu. It was supposed to be our last stop, a dingy bureaucratic government office where her last adoption paperwork would get rubber-stamped with that all-important big red star.

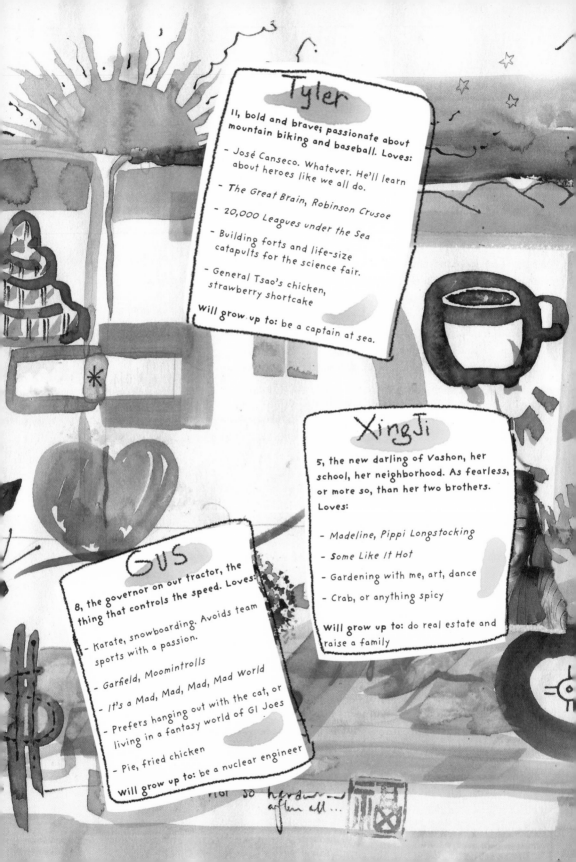

Tyler

11, bold and brave; passionate about mountain biking and baseball. Loves:

- José Canseco. Whatever. He'll learn about heroes like we all do.
- *The Great Brain, Robinson Crusoe*
- *20,000 Leagues under the Sea*
- Building forts and life-size catapults for the science fair.
- General Tsao's chicken, strawberry shortcake

Will grow up to: be a captain at sea.

XingJi

5, the new darling of Vashon, her school, her neighborhood. As fearless, or more so, than her two brothers. Loves:

- *Madeline, Pippi Longstocking*
- *Some Like It Hot*
- Gardening with me, art, dance
- Crab, or anything spicy

Will grow up to: do real estate and raise a family

GUS

8, the governor on our tractor, the thing that controls the speed. Loves:

- Karate, snowboarding. Avoids team sports with a passion.
- *Garfield, Moomintrolls*
- *It's a Mad, Mad, Mad, Mad World*
- Prefers hanging out with the cat, or living in a fantasy world of GI Joes
- Pie, fried chicken

will grow up to: be a nuclear engineer

I was about to ask her to stop drawing the self-inflicted tattoos when the boys figured out she was drawing a watch. Her newly markered strap went all the way around her tiny wrist, with a clasp. Her watch face was a mix of Chinese characters and numbers. We all wore watches back then. And Xing would, too.

During that time, it always seemed like I was in at least two places at once. When I was at the office, I was the boss whose kids were always calling her. At home, it was the other way around. The kids would have to wait—"Quietly!"—while I had the office or clients on the other end of the phone. Playing outside was the default, the norm, whenever it wasn't raining.

Ours was the house where freedom reigned, science experiments exploded, and go-carts peeled down the long, sloped driveway with a train of neighbor kids and dogs following, screaming at minor crashes or just close calls. The kids stormed in and out of the kitchen getting supplies and props for their adventures. "Mommy, Ty wants to know if we can build a bunker up near the orchard."

"Well, that depends, pal. What does he mean by a bunker?"

"Um . . . just a fort, under the big tree."

"That sounds fine, honey. Is Xingers up there with you guys?"

I was lucky to work from home a few days a week. I was often on the phone with clients or someone at the office, though. I didn't notice the mud and dirt starting to cover the carport floor. "Oh, Mom, you won't believe how cool it is!" Gus called out proudly. It didn't hit me until I saw the dirt tracks making their way into the pantry and found him grabbing cans of chili and soup.

"You guys want to come in for lunch?"

"No thanks, Mommy. We're fine." Gus was always very sweet like that. "We just need cans and stuff that will last us!"

I asked Gus to show me their bunker before provisioning. He and I walked up, across the overgrown lawn and around my modest attempts at flower beds, to the massive hundred-foot Douglas fir that's sort of the linchpin to the property. We'd just watched *The Great Escape* on a Friday Family Cuddle Night, and there they were, with their dirt and sap-smudged faces. Little Charles Bronsons, little escapee-wannabes, halfway through the tunnel-digging project.

Little Xing and much taller Tyler were both crouched inside a dugout under the fir that was almost standing height. They had tarps spread and sleeping bags stashed. Amid the roots and dirt they'd carved out shelves for their supplies, which already had small boxes of juice and packages of Goldfish. Their pickaxes, tools, and sweatshirts were scattered, with dirt piled, spread, and tracked in every direction. I was proud of them, of course. There was nothing my kids couldn't pull off. Like me, they seemed intent on making life as adventurous as possible. Plus, now we had one of those survivalist getaways—just in case we ever needed it.

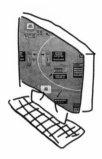

"Client server"
didn't have anything to do
with helping a customer.

"Hot linking"
didn't mean sausages.
"Pirating" was about
duplicating software —
how terribly unromantic.

A "platform" wasn't
political or even a raft
I could sail away on.

It's not like I wanted out. I was busy raising the kids and running the business. I had jettisoned my job and was back to building our film production company, Merwin Creative. It was rocking, and I was riding the roller coaster. I had the distinguished honor of being the only mom around who'd brushed Bill Gates's hair or escorted him to the restroom. Other moms made grilled cheese sandwiches or baked cookies without burning them. Me, I had other attributes.

As part of the effort to market the fledgling software industry, we got to fly all over the world and film people like Nelson Mandela, Steve Jobs, Andy Groves, Julia Roberts. We met Japanese squid fishermen praying in their ancient shrines and visited orphanages in Kolkata. We went on helicopter shoots over Hong Kong and Stockholm or shot on historic wooden schooners, on Wall Street, or Carnaby Street. Sometimes we even shot in Panavision, for God's sake, hiring symphonic composers and feature film crews.

Truth is, I didn't get to (or want to) go on many of the cool shoots. As director, David went. I stayed home, ran the business, and raised the kids. I didn't mind. It was a respite from the pace of our togetherness. Besides, I was busy writing and designing the next project, mostly stuff where I didn't have a clue what it was all about, or care.

Clients hired us to think outside the box. That was easy. I didn't know there was a box. So we impressed the corporate world with our wacky new solutions. It's almost a no-brainer to look creative to folks who aren't. But honestly, who was I impressing? We were working for Corporate America. Coming from my left-wing family, and Berkeley in the 1960s, that wasn't something to brag about. Working for big business was never something a good Unitarian/quasi-socialist hippy chick, raised on farms and schooled on communes and backpacking trails, would want to do.

It was a good life, albeit over the top and maybe spilling bunkers, car camping, sand-covered full-moon beach potlucks, ferrying and scurrying between worlds: the downtown Seattle office and our sweet Vashon Island home.

Somehow, because of, or despite, or around it all I started to dream of a raft to sail away on. I kept thinking about a real finca to escape to. None of the business and technology, or the importance that folks attached to it, made any sense to me. I wanted something that did: something tangible, or at least a plan.

2.

Hatching the Plan

Xing Ji's first summer at home, my mom came up from California eager to meet her new granddaughter. The three of us girls decided to go off for a small adventure and headed out to the coast. Beth, a good friend of my sister from high school, had opened a bed and breakfast in a split-level ranch house on the banks of the Sol Duc River. We were curious to see it. The river is world-renowned for its salmon run, and Beth's husband, Richard was in fly-fishing heaven. Just a couple of years before, they had put everything they could scrape together down on the place, escaped the rat race, and moved to Forks, six hours away in the farthest outback of Washington's Olympic Peninsula. They named their place Brightwater House and offered up rooms in it to like-minded fishermen. They had created their own small sweet world to share.

For me, Beth and Richard were living proof that you could follow your passions and still pay the bills. The place was full, running at almost capacity, within a year or two. For a gal in marketing, I couldn't believe how simple it all seemed. Beth was a counselor for the nearby Clallam Indians. Richard was an archaeologist. These guys weren't about building a brand or selling anything. "It's all just word of mouth," Beth explained. "But we're already getting folks from Germany, Japan, and Australia. All these serious fly-fishermen just tell their friends. And if anyone ever asks about the décor—like what kind of furniture we have—I figure they probably aren't the kind of folks we want. So I just tell them we're completely full."

I looked around at the place sweetly filled with thrift store finds and family hand-me-downs. What Beth and Richard knew was how to attract the right folks, so they

Cascades

Seattle

PUGET
SOUND

Vashon

HOOD
CANAL

Olympics

THE
PACIFIC

could just be themselves, everyone feeling more than comfortable—feeling connected.

I felt cozy—and inspired—as I snuggled in to read with Xing, all the while listening to the river rushing by, rolling over its stony bed. I'd always fantasized about having a motel, inn, or wilderness lodge, something one could do to get by in the country. An idea started taking shape, real, like a river rock you can jump to. And should—if you want to get to the other side.

On the long drive back to Vashon the next afternoon, between a stop for chowder and singing a CD of kids' folk songs together, I tried to share my rambling thoughts with Mom.

"Does Beth have more guts than I do? Is she smarter? I mean . . . if she can do it, can't I?"

"Well, it would be wonderful if you could do something like that, honey." Mom was trying to sound supportive. "Have a little inn. Raise the kids out in the country. But where would you even begin to look? And do you really think David would want to do that? It may not be the most practical idea right now, Corky. With all that you have going on—"

I was thirty-nine. When my mom was that age, in 1959, my father died, leaving her with four kids, two hundred dairy cows, and a part-time substitute-teaching job in Petaluma, California. I was the youngest, just under four—coincidentally, Xing Ji's age. Driving home, we let ourselves sing and daydream together as we drove the miles and hours of green and blue, the forests, mountains, and waterways of the Olympic Peninsula and the Hood Canal, back to Puget Sound, and home on Vashon.

When my father died, Mom took over at the helm of our family. Practicality probably called the shots. Raising the four of us kids on a substitute teacher's salary demanded it. In reality, Mom was as much a beatnik as she was the pragmatic daughter of Swedish immigrants—at least she leaned and danced that way, and must have looked the part to the ranch families who made up most of our community, just an hour north of San Francisco and the Beat scene. Mom was also the only single parent around. That's how it felt, anyway, growing up as her kid in Petaluma, as the 1950s turned the bend into the coming decade. She had no interest in marrying her various suitors, who apparently all asked. Mom was happy doing her thing and didn't seem to care a fig what other people thought about it. She showed us all what it is to feel the rhythm of the boogie-woogie, and the importance of the freedom to enjoy it. She listened to nascent public radio, Pacifica Radio, before the days of NPR, and subscribed to the *New Yorker* instead of a newspaper. The FBI came to our house to tell her to stop getting the *Worker's World*. She laughed them away. No one did this stuff back then, or at least not many.

There wasn't one pivotal moment when I came to think of my mother as different, as a rebel. I grew up knowing—feeling—that you didn't need to rebel if you had never been part of the norm to begin with. It wasn't just okay to be different; the whole question was irrelevant. "Just be yourself," Mom would tell me.

So: All told, maybe the decision to look for a new place, and a new life outside of the rat race, was just an odd version of my free-spirited but oh-so-practical Swedish mother's pragmatism. The sheer idea of finding a finca always drove Mom a little crazy in its impracticality. She kept hoping I'd grow out of the idea.

Poor Mom, I don't think she ever learned that saving your soul can qualify as common sense. Looking back now, across the years, I see that looking for La Finca was not only intentional, but one of the truly proactive decisions in my life. I was deliberately acting on my own behalf, like being my own guardian angel. For much of my life I have let fate have its way with me, take me where it would. But there are a handful of specific proactive moments that stand out in their clarity. They're clear both in how well I remember them and in the crystalline certainty I felt when they happened. Once I've committed, I stay true to them, as they stay true to me. They are much more than decisions. They are epiphanies that hit my heart and gut simultaneously. My head is blessedly uninvolved. Are they the rocks I step on while crossing a mountain stream? Or are they some form of signpost or milestone, reminding me where I am, or where I need to go?

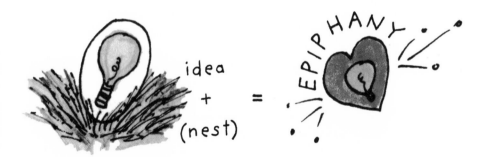

idea + (nest) = EPIPHANY

Six months after the visit to Beth's, I turned forty. David and I went away for my birthday, without the kids. Classic me: For our special getaway I chose a small-time observatory in Goldendale, Washington. I wanted it to be romantic, and I wanted David to want to see the stars as much as I did—and I wanted there to be a decent restaurant in town. It wasn't happening. The skies clouded over and there were no stars to see. So we talked. And drove. And somehow taking the curves in that old Saab around those open "Horse

Heaven Hills," and turning forty, and talking, something clicked. Something that had been forming and rattling around inside my head came out.

"Hey, David, if all these years so far we've been living a life that at least I never wanted or anticipated, how about we make a plan for something we both want for the second half? How about when we travel, instead of just being the vacationers who stay with the hip expat innkeepers in Thailand, Mexico, or Hawaii, what if, for the next ten years as we're raising the kids, we keep our eyes out for a place to escape to? Then, at the end, we become the hip expat innkeepers we're always so envious of."

He listened, and as usual I rambled on. "We could be the cute couple running the funky inn—and somewhere where it's warm! The kids would all be off at college or living their own lives by then—done with needing us year-round, at least. They'd love to come visit. You could be the dive master. David . . . ? I'd make the blueberry muffins."

I'd always dreamed of being an innkeeper, and David knew it. He was my best friend. He loved to see me happy; he also loved adventure. Funny thing is, though, I'm not much of a baker. I've never made a blueberry muffin, and I don't even like them much. I think that's what they mean about being careful what you wish for. Sometimes it's hard to recognize the difference between fantasies and goals. But then, if I'd been too careful, maybe nothing would have happened.

Vieques was too tempting to resist:

a rugged, sun-drenched, nonconformist with a Spanish accent
and palm fronds tossing like open arms...

3.

Exploring the New World

David goes for "the Plan," and we decide that for the next ten years I'll be the family's designated vacation scout. I'll choose places in search of our ultimate escape, based on two fundamental requirements: (1) We can get there on frequent-flier miles. (2) They are interesting, offbeat places, undeveloped enough that we can see ourselves living there eventually.

In other words, trips to Disneyland are not part of the program. But where to first? Mexico? I love it there, always have, but property ownership seems too complex. The Virgin Islands? No attraction, only memories of wealthy college kids darting off to St. John's for Thanksgiving. I'm not that genteel. Belize? Not enough frequent-flier miles . . . maybe next year.

I am up for adventure, as long as I can do some initial planning. In a little-known book called *Rum and Reggae: The Insider's Guide to the Caribbean,* the savvy travel author states unequivocally that some of the best beaches anywhere are on two small and virtually unknown islands, Vieques and Culebra. Huh? They were not included in most maps and guidebooks back then. How could there be Caribbean islands no one had heard of?

Just as the two islands are beginning to feel a bit like Never-Never Land and way too good to be true, we visit friends in Port Townsend, and spot a beat-up old Volvo parked with a bumper sticker that says, "I ❤ Culebra." It's a dark, wet day, but I stop.

"Kids, hang on a minute. I'll be right back."

Just like the islands, this opportunity might be too good to be true. I park the car and dash across the street in the pouring rain, leaving my card under the wiper blade with this note: "Please call me if you really know and love Culebra."

The next day a complete stranger is on the phone telling me, "Yep. It's true." He sounds like a nice guy—relaxed, savvy. "Both Culebra and Vieques are real, even though no one seems to know about them. And they're both amazing," he reassures me, "with the best beaches I've ever seen."

I'm sold. I book our flight to San Juan, Puerto Rico, for the next February, Presidents' Day 1997. From there we will take a ferry to these two "Spanish Virgins," scattered halfway between Puerto Rico and the US Virgin Islands. These mysterious islands will be the first stops in our first step on a ten-year plan. No problem—I'm a relatively patient person. Who cares if it takes a decade to find the right spot?

We were all ready and united—in those early fledgling family days, as we are today—by a common love of adventure and travel. Fun was our priority, and we were in sync, in that magic, fleeting window of time when all of us, at our varying ages, were able to agree on what was fun.

David and I had only been to San Juan once before, and then for only two hours. But you know how you can fall in love with the really cute guy in the truck next to you at the red light? How, just by his brief smile before you both drive away, you are certain it's love? It was sort of like that with Puerto Rico for me. I fell in love in the time it took to go out for dinner near the airport, during a layover, en route to St. Lucia. The restaurant was the Metropol. What hit me was more than the look or fragrances of the place. Instead it seemed the air itself was almost palpable—redolent of the island's mix of cultures, layered with tropical overtones and imbued with a cool Latin pride.

In those few hours we were there, I sensed that Puerto Ricans care a lot about things I find important—the taste of food and the grace with which you are served, lighthearted camaraderie, and not giving a hoot about pretensions, just taking it easy. It's hard to explain the odd mix of casual and totally classy, traditional and spontaneous, but that's what this place felt like. Maybe that was why it called to me and felt somehow familiar. Maybe it was just how the values lined up with my own. The music, the *pescado criollo* with black beans and rice, the waiters in guayaberas with their classic white linen shirts: Puerto Rico worked its magic on me without even trying, a brief Latin version of the red-light smile.

We were all too tired from the red-eye flight from Seattle to do much in San Juan other than dig in to what we all agreed was the best fried chicken any of us had ever had, before we took off in a plane barely big enough to seat the five of us. We were bound for Culebra, the first of our two "Spanish Virgin Island" explorations. The pilot, a Texan named Trixie, had large, bright plastic flowers in her large, bright red hair. She laughed a lot, and loudly, as she snuck the little plane through the hills of Culebra toward the notoriously narrow approach to Dewey, this small island's largest town—no, its only town. It was known among the sailing crowd for its remarkably protected harbor and the canal cutting through its center, and by everyone else for its ungodly flight path through the hills. Trixie's life-before-your-eyes-wing-scraping-the-hills landing was, and remains, one of the most memorable parts of our stay on Culebra.

Over the next few days we played on the beaches, ate at a great bagel place, snorkeled with the sea turtles, enjoyed Mexican food with the hip Culebra crowd, and even looked at property with a realtor, just to see what was there. But we weren't there for Western ways of enjoyment, so we took off, back to the main island. Lots of fun; no magic.

For the next few days the five of us toured Puerto Rico's Central Cordillera, the narrow range that forms an east–west spine down the width of the island. We stayed in an old coffee plantation that had been turned into a parador (a historic guesthouse) in Jayuya, the highest mountain area. We let the kids discover the prehistoric petroglyphs on river rocks as we cooled off from jungle treks in wild mountain streams. We toured a small Taíno museum built in the shape of a mythical creature, entering through its large gaping mouth. We visited the nearby historic home of the *independistas* who fought for their liberty against the United States. All along the way, the Puerto Rican people offered up their warm and casual hospitality.

What was it about this place and its culture? Something about it made me feel both at home and excited. In that comfortable, happy state, we went off to the final phase of this first exploratory foray for a week on Vieques, La Isla Nena—Puerto Rico's little sister island.

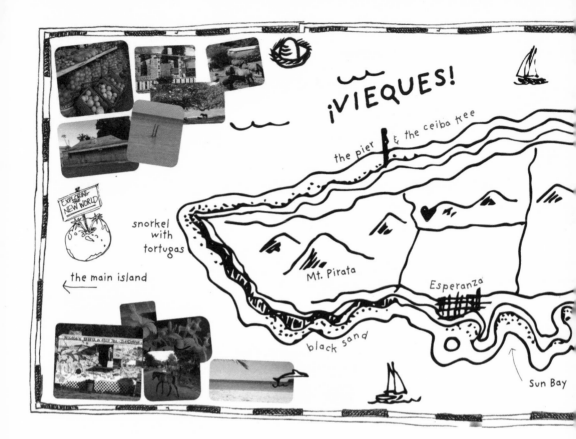

It's late afternoon when the ferry's beat-up bumper clunks into its equally beat-up dock in downtown Isabel Segunda, Vieques's largest town. Named after a fairly unpopular child Spanish queen, it is anything but regal. In the hot, bright sunshine the dock smells like fried foods, fish, and gasoline—totally funky, in other words, and to me that's a good sign.

The five of us walk, dragging and bouncing rolling suitcases over the cracked, broken, and missing sidewalks, the few blocks up the main road into town. That street is called Muñoz Rivera. My guidebook explains that Muñoz was a Puerto Rican politician, which seems normal enough. It goes on to say he was also a poet, a journalist, and a major figure in the struggle for Puerto Rican independence. I wonder, Do we have main streets named after folks like that at home? Do we have folks like that at home? No one seems to notice or mind the number of cars driving the wrong way down the tangle of one-way streets.

At least half the buildings seem suspended in a long-term state of disrepair. It's hard to say whether it's hurricane damage, tropical decay, poverty, or all of the above. Bright, gangly bougainvillea weaves its way through the ruins and around the buildings, with bits of magenta and fluorescent orange blossoms peeking out of the varying gray concrete forms. Rusty iron railings punctuate the crumbling masses of concrete

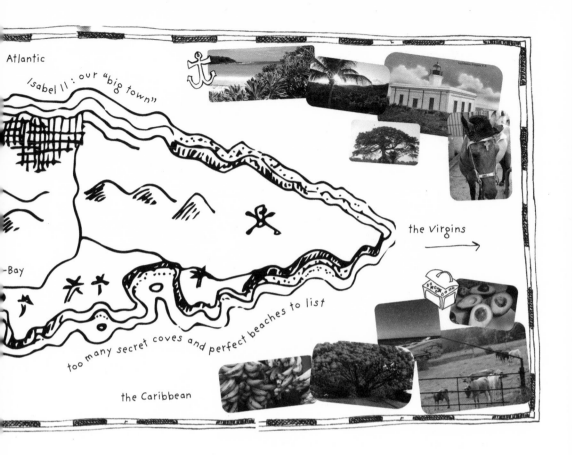

Atlantic

Isabel II: our "big town"

the Virgins →

-Bay

too many secret coves and perfect beaches to list

the Caribbean

block. The railings are beautiful, like iron lacework from an earlier, more prosperous time. Turn-of-the-century wrought-iron filigree happily living next door to art deco starbursts—odd, happy couples.

I immediately fall in love with the tiny-house-sized versions of colonial mansions. They are pink, yellow, baby blue, and trimmed in ornate wood, iron, and stonework. The paint is dirty and chipping away, showing earlier colors beneath, each filled with stories and elegant in its own way.

"It feels good," I tell David as we walk behind the kids. "I already feel more at home here." Everyone agrees. Good. Our tribe is in sync.

There are friendly stray dogs on every block. "Why are they all so small?" Gus asks. "Why are they all so weird-looking?" Ty adds.

The dogs are oddly shaped; all seem descended from some very popular chihuahua. They are as common as the cats that scurry across or laze around the broken walls, between and behind the shops and houses and vacant lots.

There are horses too, standing at the sidewalk tethered to a pole, in between parked cars in various stages of tropical rust and wear. Horses wander on their own, unbridled and seemingly unaware of the cars that make their way around them in the streets. No one bothers to honk. No one seems to be in that much of a hurry, but then we hear the

WELCOME "BIENVENIDOS" TO VIEQUES

A Tourism Pull-Out from THE VIEQUES TIMES Volume
MAP ART BY TERRY PRICE - Courtesy of La Casa del Francés - Suppleme

April 1999

OCEANO ATLANTICO

ISLA de VIEQUES

Vieques is a lovely Caribbean island located be
Puerto Rico and the U.S. Virgins, a half-hour flight
San Juan, St. Croix or St. Thomas or an hour from
Fajardo by ferry/brake. Fanned by the prevailing eas
Trade Winds it is blessed with a sub-tropical climate
marked by a mean temperature of 77° F in Decembe
and 81° F in June.

It is not an "action spot" with casinos and glitzy hi
rises but rather a peaceful place to relax and enjoy
nature's bounty. There are dozens of secluded beache
shell grounds, coral reefs, archaeological digs,

fast clatter of hooves on asphalt. Xing Ji jumps to the curb, gaping as the horse goes by. "Mommy!" she says. "It's one of those funny horses we read about!"

David, who has spent time in Colombia, had told us all about the Paso Fino lineage and the long-standing feud between Colombia and Puerto Rico: Each country claimed to be the birthplace of this breed. The intense tempo of the gallop is entirely new to us—a rapid-fire castanet-like clicking instead of the loping gait of the Western horses we are familiar with. We turn around just in time to see the rider, a young local man, racing bareback on this amazing animal, head reined in, back legs doing double time. The boy's long legs seem out of scale on the small horse. He has rounded the corner and is gone before we can think too much about it.

I've already read up on the island, enough to know that more than half of it belongs to the US Navy, and yet there's no noticeable military presence anywhere. Instead, seemingly wild horses, cows, even bulls, wander down the one-lane roads, and the roads themselves meander over and around the island. They aren't like roads back home, intent on getting from point A to point B in the most practical, efficient way. Here a road is often more just a trail, with a width of ten or twelve feet. Like a path, it can jut sharply to the left to avoid a large mango tree and then swing immediately to the right to connect to an old farm's driveway.

The roads are sometimes tree-lined and sometimes just bordered by stick and barbed-wire fences. It takes us a while to figure out that these scrawny little sticks can sprout and become large, red, peeling turpentine trees. Their trunks and limbs take on an almost human form. They line the roads, embracing each other's branches and creating canopies that feel like tunnels of leafy jungle green. Looking closer, we see where their trunks gnarl and grow around barbed wire that's been nailed to each of them many years before. These growing trees are in fact strung together! Turns out traditional fences can succumb to a hurricane, but when your fence grows into the ground, it holds up against the winds. Smart, but all pretty darn weird to us. Clearly, Vieques meets our offbeat requirements.

On our second day on the island, we are hanging out in the living room of our fancy vacation house, which looks north over the Atlantic. The kids are on the balcony, and Ty launches one of Gus's GI Joes into the sea with one of his homemade rubber band catapults. Poor Gus. After scouring the tide pools with the kids (hoping to find the diver GI Joe), we give up, come inside, and pick up the local newspaper. The most traditional thing about this double-sided, super-left-wing one-pager is its name, the *Vieques Times*. It sounds like a paper even if it doesn't look or read like one, at least not the kind we have up north. But more importantly, it has a classified section.

There we find, small as a fortune cookie, this listing: *FOR SALE: New Dawn: Women's Retreat Center.* The ad mentions something about alternative or handmade, but Tyler doesn't let me get that far. "Come on, Mom! It's perfect! We gotta go check it out! Come on, you guys!" He must be worried it might sell before we get there, if we don't hurry.

We are trying to figure out if the ride up to the hills can be worked into our daily run to the beach when Staci, the caretaker, comes in. Turns out Staci lives just across the way, up a hill and into the woods near this "New Dawn."

Staci looks like a small, wizened witch doctor, so when she says we can pick local herbs to cook with up there, that she lives with her son in a handmade open-air house, that she prefers to live without using cash, and that she hunts wild doves with slingshots to make stew, our plan is confirmed—we are going. Not sure whether we're mainly going to see the property or to pick the *recau*, or whether we just like the idea of meeting a boy in the woods with a slingshot, but soon we are on our way to Pilón. It's only seven miles out of town as the crow (or dove) flies, but it is considered way out in the boonies. Most town folk rarely head out that far, and the ones who live there try to avoid coming all the way into town, unless they really have to. Everything here is oddly reminiscent of the weird and mysterious parts of a Latin American novel, like the part where the aunt turns into a parrot and flies out the window.

The road to New Dawn is narrow and twisty, but paved. The long driveway off the road isn't, though. David bounces the beat-up rented Jeep Cherokee over small ravine-like ruts and through a small banana grove, until we get to the entrance to the property.

The gate. No matter how metaphorical it's always felt since then, it is, in fact, an actual gate. It's a long, wide, classic wooden ranch-style gate with old iron hardware, worn and welcoming. Surrounding it is a shaggy mix of spiky palms, yucca, and colorful bougainvillea. Beyond it, deep ruts cut through a packed dirt road.

This is my kind of welcome. A portal to my own funkiness; my ranch-life fantasy, my identity, my childhood, my future, my past. It is all there in an instant: who I want to be, who I am, and who I have always been. And somehow I can sort of see its history—people, weather, stories that passed through it, before me and after me. I have just found myself in the wild Latin American novel. But who am I, the aunt or the parrot? And who is writing my part?

I don't think I swore in front of the kids then, but "Oh, shit!" is all that goes through my head. I know immediately that it is a done deal, or that I want it to be.

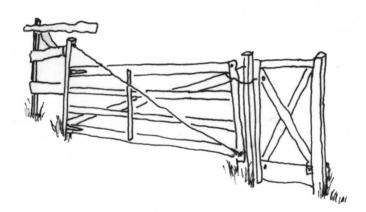

The only thing painted was the fridge

bright blue with white stars

Finding New Dawn

Gail, the owner, is as welcoming as she is notorious. Later we learn that in its twelve years, New Dawn has already become iconic, a landmark revered by adventuring women and offbeat travelers across the country. She comes out to meet us as we walk through the gate. I can tell at once, wandering in with her among the other guests, that the kids and I would be happy staying there. It is maybe a tinge grittier than even I go for, but the folks staying at New Dawn seem as relaxed and interesting as the place itself. David makes it all too clear that this is not his scene. He tends to prioritize his privacy, and it's clear that some of the women intimidate him. "Did you see the gal in the kitchen with all the tattoos and shaved head? She scares me."

"Don't be weird, Dad—she's okay!" Gus reassures him. "She introduced me to a nice dog, Phoebe."

"Whatever. We can wander around, look at the property and even consider buying it, but we aren't going to stay there." He's double and triple checking—I know that.

We walk the property with Gail, each of us carting around our own Robinson Crusoe fantasy. With nothing but jungle at its edge to define it, New Dawn's three acres seem larger than I'd expected, and the land lusher than the rest of the island. It sits in the middle, in fact maybe saddling the low hills that run the length of the island east to west. This specific pass through the hills is known as Barrio Pilón, "the bowl of the mortar and pestle." The property is cleared of the rather scrappy dry jungle that blankets much of Vieques, offering expansive views to the south, the Caribbean. From the higher hills that surround the property one could no doubt see north, to the Atlantic, as well. As expansive as the views are, the place somehow feels sheltered and hidden away. Having driven from Isabel in the north, and now gazing across this stretch to the south, I can tell we are just about halfway between the two coasts.

"Yep, you can walk to either side of the island," Gail offers. "Three miles south to Esperanza, a mile and a half to the airport. Gets sort of warm if you wait too long. But either is perfect for an early morning walk and swim. In the early days, the road wasn't paved, of course. And we didn't have any phone service, or many cars, so we rode bikes or our horses to a phone booth. It was tough in the rainy season. And hard to get all the tools and equipment we used to clear the land.

"You know, it was all jungle, just like that," and she points to the neighboring hills, "before we got here."

My head is spinning. Talk about an unbeaten path. The drama and mystique of the place matches its beauty.

Large, beautiful trees and shrubs ring its edges and dot the small pasture, punctuating various corners. "These two flamboyant trees will bloom in the summer. You know, the trees you see in all the Puerto Rican paintings, with their amazing orange blooms," Gail explains.

The romance of seeing a flame tree up close and personal does not escape me. I don't know a thing about tropical landscaping, but having read the book, I always wanted to see the actual "Flame Trees of Thika."

The landscaping is a perfect swirl of lovingly manicured and wild-ass chaos. The array of tropical leaves forms a textured green backdrop to pink impatiens, yellow ginger flowers, and the orange-red birds of paradise. Red, apricot, and light pink hibiscus are

tree-sized; bromeliads and coleus cover whole flower beds; and twin massive rubber trees support a wide woven hammock right in the middle of the front lawn. The kids are in heaven, climbing trees and chasing lizards that dart and scurry among the leaves. The wildness of it all is somehow comforting. There are secret places in the bamboo, and shrines with shells and coral bits. Offerings, no doubt—and clearly the gods have smiled back. There is an enormous old heavy-gauge iron sugar kettle—a relic from an old mill, long abandoned—used as a trough for the horses. It must weigh well over a ton. It's anyone's guess how it got here.

Emerald-bellied hummingbirds dart in and about the bananas trees surrounding the main house. A large birdcage hangs on the front porch, with two parakeets happily twittering away. A handful of dogs and cats greet us lazily as we pass them in their various napping spots. Just like the guests, reading and swinging in hammocks, everyone—human and animal—is friendly and seems part of a club I want to belong to. This is Swiss Family Robinson, without the Disneyland—a life-sized organic Candyland. I sigh with contentment, trying to stay calm.

Gail's voice cuts into my daydream. "In addition to the main house, which has six guestrooms, there's the family cabaña. Here are a few tent sites, and there are also eight ten-dollar-a-night bunks in the bunkhouse," Gail says. "It's for folks who don't want all the amenities when they travel."

It becomes clear that some guests stay for weeks, maybe months, on end. She is clearly proud of the community she has led the charge in creating. "Plenty of folks got their first introduction to Vieques through New Dawn. Whether it's coming down for a

vacation or taking one of our carpentry classes for young women, that's been a win-win thing for sure. They come down from the States and help build the place."

With a massive wraparound porch and the countless doors that open onto it, it's hard to know exactly when you are inside or out—or if that matters. It's clear that almost all of the furniture is made in the same two-by-four New Dawn "style." Anyone who knows carpentry and looks up to see the rafters would be puzzled, amused, or aghast. The lasting evidence of the unique building style and rafter-and-joist spacing technique entertains guests to this day. But, heck, who are we to judge? It's all still standing after Hurricane Hugo's infamous seventeen-hour pummeling seven years before our first visit.

Gail casually ushers us inside to wander through the main house. "When people say the place seems a little funny for a guesthouse or a business," she goes on, "I always tell them this wasn't designed to be an inn. It was built as our family's home."

That helps explain things. I duck around the large television set and step over the futons in the lobby area. As much as I like both Guatemalan fabric and futons, I'd like to imagine the place without any of them.

The six bedrooms upstairs are barracks-like, outfitted with a unique Quonset hut–style PVC rigging for custom-made mosquito netting stretched tight over the beds, each with its own faded Guatemalan bedspread. The massive furniture, like the walls and floors, is bare, unpainted wood. Simple. Downright drab. Not much color anywhere—but I can fix that.

I notice there isn't a bathroom—as they say, a shared bathroom—down the hall. Nope, but there is a sink in the hallway, and someone, a guest I'm guessing, is brushing their teeth and nods a friendly hello as we walk by. The one toilet downstairs does have walls. I'm not sure why, but the walls only reach up to about six feet, three-quarters of the way to the ceiling. The rest of the walls simply aren't. Just open air. And if that isn't wild and crazy enough, the original lumber the women had built the simple board walls with has shrunk over the years, enough that there are significant—say, quarter-inch—gaps large enough to look through and see whether the restroom is free or not. This is the kind of thing that the kids notice and adore.

"Remember, it was built as their home," I whisper to David. Like that somehow makes it less weird.

David rolls his eyes. "Don't worry, honey," I say. "We can finish those walls, and I can make everything all bright and pretty. I'll paint the furniture and make my floor art rugs—like I do at home."

Like I said, he trusts me.

Trust or not, David is a businessman. Like me, he can't help but ponder the value of things, the potential. We both see the value of this virtually unknown island's almost endless, almost empty, certainly undeveloped, white sand beaches and coral reefs. Not value as in the dollars we want to make on it. No, it's the importance of its rarity in this well-traveled, overdeveloped world. How has Vieques managed to escape being ruined? How long before it is? Just how scared should we be about the navy's presence? Why isn't it on any maps? Over the years I've learned and developed a variety of theoretical answers. But back then all I wanted to know was "Honey, can we afford it?"

We wrap our visit up but haven't gotten very far down the road when David starts in. "If we do this crazy thing, we're absolutely putting in a pool, closing down the restaurant and bar, and getting all the cars and trucks to park on the driveway and off the grass that had turned to dirt. Oh, and that bunkhouse for eight people, we're turning that into a nice cabin for two. We'll make the same money, but reduce the number of folks milling around."

I liked that. Fair enough, and smart to boot. We decide to go down to the beach— Navio, the kids' favorite for bodysurfing. The kids will be entertained and we can talk.

David and I are making a mental list by the time we park. "Just how much business do we have to bring in every month to pay the mortgage and the bills? And what friends should we ask—who might want to be in on this deal?"

While the kids are busy playing in the water, we're looking for something to write on, doing the math in our head, trying to line out the monthly "nut." It's clichéd to say our contract was written on a cocktail napkin. Ours is on a paper towel, and it isn't a contract—it is David doing the numbers. He comes up with a worst-case scenario showing that even without friends, and even if things go south, we might be able to take a second mortgage on our house.

At that point I really didn't know what a second mortgage was, but if he said we could do it, that was good enough for me. My God, how I trusted that man. Years later, I'd pay a price for that unconditional, blind trust. But he, too, must have trusted me and my gut feeling: that we were supposed to do this.

Tyler is at least as adamant as I am. He jumps up and down. "I'll do anything!" he shouts. "Anything! If we can just buy it." I wonder where Ty's vision of all this comes from. He too is seeing beyond the ultra-funk factor to something else. I think David's fantasy is to provide a way for my dream to come true. Gus is clearly interested in the trees he can climb all over the property, and Xing loves the tropical flowers and the nice people she stops and chats with, but she is equally fixated on her beloved American Girl doll Matilda's nap schedule. My fantasy is clear: I want to be the wacky innkeeper of a cool place. Maybe Ty was Robinson Crusoe in an earlier life, and the tropical treehouse nature of New Dawn calls to some ancient memory. "I'll go to the Catholic school, I'll wear a uniform if I have to!" I have no idea why Ty thinks that will help sway us.

It's odd I didn't recognize my own adventuresome trust-in-the-universe quotient by then.

Weren't we the folks who walked into an orphanage in China with two kids and came out with three, hitchhiked halfway across the country, rafted whitewater rivers for our honeymoon?

I never saw myself as reckless, still don't.

It's not until now, halfway through my fifties, that I can look back and see myself a bit more clearly. Now I know that I am, and always have been, comfortable taking risks.

None of us had any idea of the role this place would have in our lives. I see now just how much love and trust David showed by helping us buy the place. Years later, as I was talking with guests on the deck one evening, a jazz singer from New York sang "Moonlight in Vermont" out under the stars. Everyone was moved by the magic of the moment. She asked me about David. "Tell me about your ex-husband. I'm thinking he must have been quite a character."

I assumed that, like most other women, she wanted to hear the sad details of the divorce and shattered dreams, how and why he left.

"No, I meant I want to know more about a husband who would do this for a wife," she said. "There aren't that many who help, or even let, their wives follow their dreams, especially adventures like this. What sort of husband goes with his wife to buy a tropical inn in the Caribbean when they live in Washington State, while they are in the middle of raising kids? He must be a special guy. He must have loved and trusted you so much."

I loved the way her words opened my heart. "Yes. He was, and yes, he did."

Over the course of the first week on Vieques we kept plotting and figuring how we could manage to do this. Ty was old enough to babysit, so we would leave the kids with a Monopoly game and their GI Joes and go out for a date night—which meant business strategy at the Crow's Nest, a nearby guesthouse, bar, and restaurant where we'd sort of gotten to know the bartender Mark. We were adding up our own risk tolerance, as well as our savings. The owner, Liz—a contemporary and good friend of Gail's—sat at the bar with us, and the two of them encouraged us. "Go for it!" she said. "All that place needs is a good cleaning up, a pool, and smart folks running it."

Hmm . . . Two out of three?

During the day we head to the beach for more strategizing. I dig my toes into the fine white powder. I've lived near the ocean most of my life: from northern California, land of crashing waves and undertow, to Alaska's steely, cold Cook Inlet. I'm lucky enough to have lived on the Côte d'Azur for a while as a teenage nanny, and to have traveled to Hawaii, Mexico, and Southeast Asia. I live on an island in the middle of gentle Puget Sound. I know beaches in their varying forms, but I've never seen beaches like this. Nothing like this clean white sand, impossibly turquoise blue water, and azure sky. Where the two blues meet at the horizon, the colors are sharp enough to almost clash.

The high salt content of the Caribbean makes you so buoyant you can lie down on the water and float. I am unused to its almost tideless calm. This beach, whose official name is Media Luna, we call "Baby Beach." The water slides in and out with barely a ripple. A day here is like playing in a tropical bathtub. Farther out in this protected bay you can play in its mellow version of waves.

As we are all playing in the water, David shouts, "And we have to change the name!"

I know that. We are both in marketing, after all.

"The *Finca*!" he shouts in between waves. "We've been looking for our finca for how long now?"

"That's perfect!" I yell from my side of the swelling surf. "Just La Finca! The farm. The getaway! I love it!"

But David is smarter still. "Nope," he bounces back. "Too generic. You're going to want a name that identifies the place. La Finca could be anywhere from Tijuana to Tierra del Fuego."

And so it is born, conceptually at least: La Finca Caribe, our Caribbean country getaway, retreat, farm—it is all those. It will be our escape, assuming that it can even happen, that we can pull it off. Heading back to our overly full lives—four thousand miles away, where everything is gray and green and sort of wet, with the kids and the clients and the pets and the book groups, the Unitarian Sunday school, Mandarin lessons, and sports, I'm wondering how. How—now seriously, *how on earth*—are we going to squeeze the purchase, not to mention the actual ongoing management of the place, into our lives?

I don't remember if anything actually went wrong, or if it was just the fear that something might, but I cry on the ferry as we leave in the morning sun. We have to leave the finca and the island. We will try to put together an offer for Gail in the weeks ahead, when we are back. I sit on the boat's stern watching Vieques get smaller and smaller on the horizon. I am afraid it will disappear forever and the whole place, the whole idea, and the whole week will end up being one of those stories you share around the campfire.

We really know nothing of the climate, the culture, the history of the island, not to mention the local tourism or the hospitality industry. "Did I ever tell you about the time I seriously considered buying a place on a little island in the Caribbean? No, *really*!

We almost did . . ." Like flipping the raft in Horn Creek, or fainting in the Hmong Village in the Golden Triangle, this latest adventure might fade into the ho-hum of a coulda, shoulda, woulda or be at best an entertaining dinner party anecdote.

And so I cry, alone on the boat deck, heading back to our lives. Away from what I desperately want my life to be, the road I want to take. I realize it's crazy to dream that big. It's impossible, I think—let it go. I have three busy kids to get off of this boat, into a taxi van, and onto the long flight. Home. Say goodbye to brilliant and bright, warm and breezy. Say goodbye to what might have been. Wipe the tears away; don't let the kids see you crying.

Over the rest of the winter and spring, amid school lunches and running to ferries, the silly escape notion won't go away. David is afraid, of course. We both are. I know he feels responsible for making the numbers, bringing home the bacon, just as I feel responsible for our cooking it right and maintaining our happy home life. Something like this could be disastrous for the family.

The finca is on our minds all the time. I think about it as we commute together on the ferry, to the office and back to Vashon. I think about it in client meetings. I think about it as I read to the kids. "I can't tell if this would be the smartest, or the stupidest thing, we've ever done," David worries aloud from time to time. "I just wish we could find one of our friends to go in on it with us. Like we did with the boat."

Eyeing fellow commuters—friends and neighbors—we join their table and start our pitch. You would think in that cold, gray-scale color of winter ferry rides, folks would want in on a tropical escape fantasy. But they never do. No one quite believes we have really found an undiscovered island in the Caribbean, rimmed in long, white, empty beaches with herds of wild horses, few roads, and no resorts or traffic lights.

We get serious about the plotting and planning. If they won't join us, we'll have to do it on our own. The gods favor us with more and more work from Microsoft. David runs the numbers again. We can borrow against our house. Heck, Gail is financing the deal herself. We don't even need a bank. Gulp. It becomes clear that we really can do it. From finding the place to financing it, it is happening about a decade earlier than we ever expected. When I cooked up that little plan for our expat working retirement, I thought it might take a handful of years, not months.

David and I know how to pull together projects, so we do. For the next ten years, until the kids are out of high school, we will hire folks to stay on site and run the place. We are confident that we'll find adventurous friends of friends who will line up to manage the place. As a family, we will get down there for all school holidays and summer vacations—at least for June, which is still rainy in the Northwest. When the kids are launched, we'll run it ourselves. At least for half the year, the busy half—high season, from Christmas to April. That's the plan.

On a deeper level, I have visions for the place. I see clearly what a value it will be for the community. I'm not sure how, but I can sense the importance, and joy, of sharing it with Puerto Rican kids who haven't had a chance to experience this sort of simple living. As I roll over in bed at night between dreams, I see feminist history workshops for local high school girls providing alternative life choices to teen pregnancy and marriage, and I start planning the curriculum for green living retreats for elementary kids from San Juan. This is going to be fun. And good.

the cabaña
from the pool.

Four months later, on June 16, 1996, all five of us arrive back on Vieques. Our new island. We stay in the main house, our new house. *It sure is big. And a little different than I remembered*, I think to myself, as I look around at all that needs doing.

"Let's just sign!" David says. He is enthusiastically supportive. It's our very first afternoon, and we are all together with Gail, the attorneys, and lots of wild bouquets: flowers from the property she has picked to welcome us. I am so impressed that Gail is generous enough to throw in the big glass vase that holds them, the old brass candleholders, and the Guatemalan tablecloths. She is even going to give us all the cool

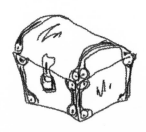

stuff in the shed, including the camping gear, if we want it. Smart woman, that Gail. I am too giddy to ask to look inside the shed before I agree. That is the least of our worries. We are signing the contract, and signing up for a life of unanticipated horizon-stretching, mind-bending craziness.

5.

On Our Own

*O*ur first hands-on stint commences that day and will last a month. Talk about on-the-job training. Funny thing, though—the only one on hand to do the training is the finca itself. She's my new boss and teacher. We will all learn over time to be comfortable letting the finca be in charge. And she is, regardless.

There are no guests on the books for now. The plan is for the kids and me to get things cleaned up and ready for our new caretakers to get settled and up to speed. David is staying with us for the first week and then taking off for work, a film shoot in Philadelphia for Microsoft.

I don't remember the wild horses looking this thin, even desperate. Maybe it's the weather. The island is in the middle of a long, hot drought. The air is thick with a chalky yellow haze.

"Just the summer dust blowing in, off the Sahara," neighbors explain, trying to reassure us.

Huh? How would the Sahara have anything to do with us here? I have no problem being called a gringa here. In Alaska, newcomers are called cheechakos. I'd been one there for years, so I'm okay being a greenhorn here. But the frequency with which it occurs is unsettling.

Our first week is pure fun, just letting it all soak in. When David is gone, there is a lot less barbequing, a lot more mac-and-cheese. The kids don't mind. They know our daily trips to the beach will be shorter, know we have to get to work now. That's our deal.

The kids and I have a lot to do and learn in the next month. Because the main house doesn't have normal things like doors and windows, we find that the

Swiss Family Finca

Adobo
Recaito
Sofrito
All new thing

Even the rice is
different.

Rosie Perez
says:
"You may not
be born in
Puerto Rico,
but Puerto Rico
is definitely
born in you."
I'm getting it...

drought-starved feral cats and dogs walk right into the kitchen to ravage the trash and eat anything they can find—like dry Bisquick out of the box. A trail of the stuff winds its way across the dead grass, heading off toward the jungley edge of the property. But we're quick learners. We hoist the giant garbage can on top of the fridge and weigh it down with the large conch shells that adorn nearly every deck rail and shelf.

As hot and dry as it is, happily there is, for both my relief and relative disbelief, this magical expanse of turquoise known as the Caribbean Sea. Everything seems too different to be true. But there it is, this sea—to wake up to, to turn to throughout the day—stretching out to the south, all the way to South America, and to the past, to pirates and plunderers.

No longer are trade winds some romantic notion out of books. They are my daily companions. They knock over chairs and blow papers off the desk. If we don't want to lose a reservation, we'd better weigh it down with a chunk of coral or one of those conch shells. The winds play extreme Fifty-Two Pick-Up with any deck of cards the kids leave out overnight, spreading them across the wooden deck and into the trees. On any given day or hour, the wind can range from a light breeze to an all-out blow. It's almost constant, and reliable enough to dry all our line laundry. On the windward-facing southeast corner of the house, bedsheets hang and flap, sometimes horizontally, like floral sails from Goodwill. High above the sea, and the hills rolling down to it, the laundry deck is like the bow of a ship. No, the Caribbean and its trade winds are no longer abstract notions, but they are still romantic. Everything is. And unreal.

The to-do list keeps growing and getting misplaced. Screw it. I just do everything.

Remembering that Gail showed us a shed full of things we might need, I figure I better check it out. There might be tools we could use. It might be full of treasures!

Turns out it is full—of junk, from floor to hot metal ceiling, a decade's worth of old guests' abandoned sleeping bags, long-emptied daypacks and duffels, and other stuff decayed beyond recognition. Any conceivable treasures have been carted away long ago. Even the shed itself is rotting away. *Be careful what you say yes to, cheechako.*

Note to self: Everything in the tropics can rust, rot, or just disappear. Unfortunately, the stuff in the shed hasn't disappeared, and we need to get rid of it all. It's 95 degrees Fahrenheit outside, so the shed is like an oven, and we are baking in it. Amazingly, the kids jump into the job without complaining. We are all in this together, like the Swiss Family Robinson washing up on the beach.

I am learning quickly, but not quickly enough to know how to respond when Xing Ji comes up with a baseball hat full of treasures she found in the shed. "Look how cute, Mommy!" She holds out her sunhat like an Easter basket, proudly presenting me with my first-ever rat's nest—literally, a pile of squirming baby rats. Tiny, hairless versions of the creeps I've been busy trying to get rid of and clean up after. Who knows how she got them into her hat.

"Can I keep them? *Please*, Mommy!"

I have no idea what I say, or what to do with them.

The next day I am tackling the outside bar area cupboards. They need to be cleaned out and a handle is broken. Until I have someone handy here to fix it, I'm thinking, I can just jerry-rig a duct-taped fix to this latch. Just at the moment when the roll is dangling from the tape and I'm trying, with both hands, not to let it twist around and stick to itself like it always does, the cupboard door swings open. From deep within the darkness an army of cockroaches the same size as those baby rats charges me. I think they are carrying small bayonets. I don't know. I don't look that long. The cupboard, long neglected, is filled with them—dozens, hundreds. Once exposed to light they go crazy, crawling—fast—everywhere. I slam the door and look for rubber gloves without holes. I am at the helm now, owning and running an inn in the Caribbean, but I am far, far from home and anything familiar. I've gotten us into something big here, and somehow I have to figure out how to clean that cupboard and make it all work.

I'm beginning to feel more than a little overcome with tasks when the phone rings. Someone actually wants to make a reservation! A lovely, friendly woman wants to rent the entire main house (money!) for a bunch of girlfriends. "Great!" This means we are actually in business. Or will be next year—turns out they want to book early. Oh well, with any luck we'll still be here . . . hard to say. Chances are we'll need the cash then as much as we do now.

Back then it was different. The internet was really just barely emerging. These folks didn't find us online; that term didn't even exist yet. Most likely they saw a flier on a co-op bulletin board or read an ad in some women's newsletter. Or heard about it from a friend. Whatever—right on!

Within a day or two, the phone rings again. It's a couple from the main island, Puerto Rico, who want the casita for their honeymoon next month. Great, again! A honeymoon for our first guests feels like a good omen. We'll be back in Washington by then, but who cares? I realize I have to become comfortable leaving guests, and the whole place, in the hands of our caretakers.

Through neighbors on Vashon we find a young adventurous couple, Bruce and Louise, who sign up for the job. Should we call them managers or caretakers? I wonder about the difference. Oh, well. They're qualified, they want the job, and they've lived in the tropics. As part of their qualifications in their interview, they tell us how a few years earlier they apparently, sort of accidentally, joined a cult on a small island somewhere in the South Pacific. They describe a harrowing escape that involved long-distance ocean swimming and small planes doing emergency nighttime takeoffs and landings.

Somehow, in my forty-year-old mind, this qualifies them to be our first caretakers.

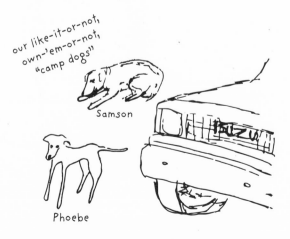

our like-it-or-not, own-'em-or-not, "camp dogs"

Samson

Phoebe

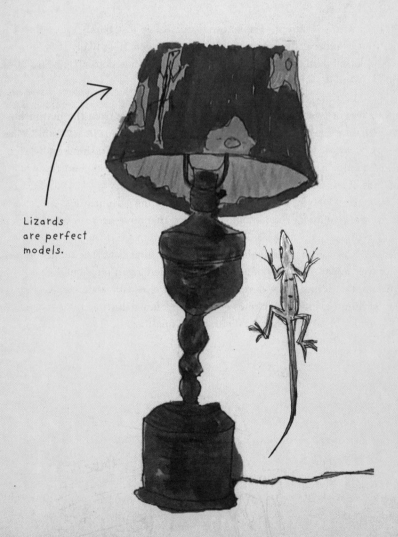

Lizards
are perfect
models.

new fruit to get used to

A Month of Firsts

The storm waits until after David leaves. The shudder of the house is the first clue something is wrong. Not a tiny shimmy, like I've felt houses do before. This is akin to a dog shaking off water at the beach. The massive main house moves. What does it take to make a whole house do that? Before I can ponder that for too long, a white plastic deck chair scoots across the deck. Ty, an avid snowboarder, shouts, "Whoa! That one copped air!"

"Grab them!" I command, like I'm in charge. I am, actually. "We have to get these doors closed!"

What was it Gail told me about having to close the doors for hurricanes and tropical storms? Otherwise the main house doors are almost never closed. Our doors aren't doors, anyway—they are heavy lumber shutters without handles, knobs, or locks. To keep them from blowing open we have to brace a two-by-six across two interior galvanized brackets. But where are those boards?

"Ty, quick—help me check under the outside bar for those boards. Gus, Xingers, get upstairs and crank every window in every bedroom closed!"

We are scrambling. The kids love it. It's not every day you get to see chairs fly. Every chapter of *Endurance* and *Robinson Crusoe* we've read aloud is coming to life. The rain is blowing in sideways. The winds are howling as the skies darken.

They love being commanded. "Aye, aye, Mother-bird!" Gus salutes as he takes off on his mission. "Roger that!" Ty is gone. Into the wild.

These days any important activity the boys do is prefaced by odd SWAT-team-like hand gestures to each other. The things movie guys do. I don't know if they understand what they're saying to each other, but they seem to. Ty and I search the deck and bar, a kind of workbench filled with weird stuff we rifle through as quickly as we can. We don't mind getting wet—this isn't the cold rain of home. Besides, the kids get to be heroes. They are my heroes, for sure. We finally find the boards around the other side of the house under a table on the laundry porch area, which is on the windward, and wetter side, and batten down the hatches and live to tell the tale. We feel victorious.

"A whole bunch of the window crank things don't work, Mom. But we got 'em mostly closed by pressing on each of the glass panels. There's like five or six in every window."

"Good thinking, Guster. Sounds like we'll be mostly dry." I go to fix something to eat, all the while wondering why the gals didn't bother replacing those handle cranks. Another thing for the to-do list, I guess. But for now I'm happy that I can add a few carrots and scramble an egg into some Top Ramen for dinner. We'll ignore the MSG and call it good. "Come on, kids. Let's eat before we go to bed. We may lose power."

Outside the storm is going strong, but we have drawn a line between outside and in. It feels weird inside with everything closed, even at night, because the whole place is usually so open. It feels like a birdcage with a cover on it. But we are safe and sound, and only a little wet. It's interesting to live without a dryer. *God, I hope there wasn't anything on the line.*

A hot shower would feel great, but we don't have one of those either. Our showers are early models of passive solar water heating and are all outside. We spread things out on chairs and tables to dry and get into bed slightly damp, feeling sure we're on top of things.

I sleep alone in Room 3, the southeasternmost of our rooms. It feels like the bow of a ship facing straight into the storm. It gets the first leak. Leaks. The ping-plop of a drip, then another.

"Mom! There's a leak in my room." Sounds like Ty in Room 1. Xing Ji chimes in, "There's another one over my bed in here!" Room 5. That means both sides of the roof. The kids and I each have our own room, so we apparently each have our own leaks. We need pots, fast, to catch the water. That means going downstairs. The power is out now, so there's no light.

"Kids, see if you can pull your beds away from the windows. Ty, help Xing." Without that nudge, three-foot-tall Xing would be pushing and dragging a queen-size finca bed, which was no doubt made by our predecessors out of four-by-fours and heavy plywood and weighs a ton. Gotta protect that girl from herself. Gotta do a lot of things. Gotta get my muumuu on and go downstairs and find those pots.

This is the pivotal point—where you learn not to be afraid of the bugs you might be stepping on as you run down the hall, down the stairs, and across the main living area. Right as I'm scrabbling for pots and pans in the dark kitchen, I realize I'm barefoot. And I'm about to run back up those stairs, where just this afternoon I saw at least one of those long black centipedes curled in the corner. Oh, well, what the heck. I am Isak Dinesen, or I will be eventually. I am a pioneer in the outback. I am invincible, or so I

"And above all, watch with glittering eyes the whole world around you because the greatest secrets are always hidden in the most unlikely places. Those who don't believe in magic will never find it."

—Roald Dahl

try to convince myself as I run back up in the dark, scared out of my wits of crunching or squishing something underfoot.

We get pots and pails in place and go back to bed. With all that's going on outside, we're not too bothered by the drops plopping into them, though Ty's leak is more like a stream. Hopefully the kids can sleep, but I can't. I've entered the anger phase. I am furious—I'll sue Gail. Is there a lemon law for houses? Can we get our money back? She had to know about these leaks! I am incensed. And I am so embarrassed. They had been right, all those folks back home who said I was crazy. What the hell was I thinking? I move from anger to sadness. What have I done to our family? Our kids will never go to college or get jobs because I have squandered our hard-earned savings on this ridiculous, impossible endeavor. I've bought a lemon. I'm not Isak Dinesen; I am a joke.

Oh, the remorse. It's way too hard doing this alone. I convince brave Xing Ji, who's been much more amused than concerned about it all, that she'll sleep better curling up in my bed with me. Together we doze off.

Early the next day, remarkably, the sun rises in its usual place, that same southeast corner. The long night has ended. I step outside with my morning tea to view the damage. Amazingly, the worst that happened is that we missed grabbing another deck of cards, which is now plastered on leaves throughout the woods. There's an eight of spades shellacked to a philodendron leaf the size and shape of an elephant's ear. And I can't help but notice that the lawn around the house—scraggly yellow grass, suffering from the recent long dry spell—now has a faint wash of green, as if a massive watercolor brush has been at work in the wild night while we slept. Everything is wet and sparkly, already drying out in the morning's steamy warmth. There's a new smell to the place—earthy. The island seems to have been brought back to life.

We spend a month at La Finca that first summer. Like going deep when we snorkel, we want to dive in, get wet and salty and sandy, get to know it all. Our neighborhood is the jungle and hills that surround us, the island, town, the beaches. But our three acres alone prove to be a whole new world to get to know. Something odd, between magic and quirkiness, starts to reveal itself. The place has a natural beauty that's evident as soon as you walk through the gate, but this is something more than that. There's something else embedded in the property and its handful of funky wooden buildings.

You can sense the histories and adventures that have taken place. It's almost like the love that has gone into the place shines back out, asks for more. Like a beloved dog that wants more petting and won't ever have enough. In addition to the main house, the one we call Casa Grande, there are three cabins: the bunkhouse, the funkiest of all, where caretakers live; the casita, a former toolshed in the bamboo; and the crazy, tall family cabaña. None of them have hot water. Heck, back then only one had a toi-

let. Caretakers and guests have
to walk to the main house or the
bathhouse next to the outside
showers. Guests don't seem to
mind. Like us, they don't come
for normal. Each has its own to-
tem, its own token of past love
and creativity—nothing planned
or contrived, just relics of some
creative endeavor.

In one cabin there's a wild
mosaic frame made of petite
blue-and-white tiles, with a small
mirror left of center poking out
of wild jagged edges. The family
cabaña has a beautiful, handmade '70s-style stained-glass
window. Upstairs in the main
house, high above the stairwell,
someone has cut stars out of what
would have been a plywood wall.

One day I hear, "Gus! Get
up here! Quick!" Outside Tyler
is commanding the troops' at-

Room 3 ♡

tention—he's great at that. "I've found someone buried underneath the trees by the
cabaña." That one even gets my attention.

"What do you mean by someone, honey?" I call as we scramble over to Ty, wanting
to confirm that this time he's exaggerating and we don't have an unsolved murder on
our hands. Before he can answer, we make it to the fence line to find him kneeling on
the ground, peeling back vines and dead leaves. "Check this out!" he says.

Gus and Xing start to help with the unearthing, which reveals a long, naked body, a
woman made of concrete and stone. She's lying peacefully in the earth, arms and hands
folded around her belly, which is piled with shells and rocks and blanketed with dainty
green groundcover. She's beautiful and at rest.

"Is someone really in there?" Xing wonders. We decide to leave her be and get back
to work.

"Oh, no, that's just Gaia, the earth mother goddess," Gail explains the next time she
stops by. "Just a shrine in her honor some of us made a few years back."

I've decided Gail has been generous after all. She left these treasures—the woven
lamps, the bedspreads, and an amazing Old Alaskan hand-cranked ice crusher. "Don't
bother using a blender for the margaritas and all the other icy blended drinks folks will

want. Grinding ice destroys them, but nothing can hurt this guy. That's why I'm leaving it for you and the bar. It really belongs to the place."

Around the corner from the long-neglected bar, now a work project area, is the front door, where an antique sewing machine is nested in a flower bed. It's almost overtaken by the philodendron and spiderwort climbing over it. Farther back there's a six-foot stretch of wrought iron, a filigree remnant of an old plantation gate that braids its way through the bougainvillea. Along our front fence line, an old iron bed is woven into the barbed-wire fence. Best of all, up in the horse pasture there's an enormous antique iron sugar urn. It's filled with trailing plants, at least half weeds now, but it's beautiful.

I delight in my role as steward of these relics and creative inspirations. I want to be someone who finds or makes these treasures. I want to know their histories. I think the personal facet of these items helps our guests feel more at home than they would at any regular inn. The handful of folks who stay with us in the first few weeks feel more like friends than hotel guests—as though they're part of the place or, like me, want to be. They want to be worthy of the place; they want to pet this "loving dog."

Xing Ji's sixth birthday is coming up. How do I pull off a celebration amid all that we have to do? Two young college women staying in the main house offer to help. They'll make cupcakes. Another guest paints a small terra-cotta pot in blue and green flower designs and plants a tiny fuzzy cactus in it. Surprise! Xing is thrilled. Her big sister "aunties" surround her. She's soaking up the attention and considers the furry cactus something of a pet.

Everyone seems to want to help, even with the big chores that need doing—the cleaning, the repairs. We are all in this together, this first month of opening La Finca Caribe, like the crew from the SS Minnow on Gilligan's Island.

Gus and Ty take hammer and nails and start

building a treehouse in the turpentine trees. When a few boards are in place, Mario—the gardener we'd inherited with the place—calls a halt. He knows all of the trees and warns the kids out of the enormous rubber tree and the mangoes as well. Frustrated but rarely daunted, they shift their focus to ensuring a steady supply of coconuts by building a ladder up the trunk of a palm tree. I'm sure the tree doesn't appreciate the boys nailing boards into it, but that doesn't stop it from growing any—the boys use that ladder for years. (Although the ladder is still there today, it starts about twenty-five feet off the ground. Its rungs, first built for the reach of young boys, have stretched several feet apart. Just one of the things guests ask about as they tour the place, twenty years later: "What's up with those boards way up there on that one palm tree?")

Our own little magical additions carry on the tradition and make this place ours at the same time. But the quirkiness isn't all sweet and good, nor is it bad. It's just weird. Every day is a reminder that things are different here. Odd things happen.

Without warning, the municipal water supply goes out. Zip. Shut off. That doesn't happen at home. Not for a couple days at a time, anyway. Vieques's main water supply comes from El Yunque National Forest, which covers the mountains of northeastern Puerto Rico. The water is piped in under seven miles of open ocean, where the Caribbean meets the Atlantic. So breaks aren't all that rare. But of course this happens the week our first large group arrives.

Eight women from the Midwest who do all kinds of adventure travel together have taken over the main house. We love adventure travelers. It's not long before we exhaust our backup supply in the cistern. "I'm afraid you guys will have to bathe in the pool," I tell Mauve, my main contact with the group.

"No problem," she says. "As long as we don't have to drink it as well—or do we?" We buy large jugs of bottled water to drink. Take buckets and pails down to the pool. We're good to go. What next?

I'm at the desk in the main lobby. Calling it a lobby makes it sound like a real hotel. But it is the main room in the main house, and we do have a front desk bound by woven mats or palm fronds and two file cabinets that are almost rusted shut. It takes a screechy pull to open them, and when you do, you find files of musty, dusty papers in file folders and reams of old menus, old business licenses, brochures for women's retreats and travel companies.

It's not that Gail and her crew were awful housekeepers. I will learn later how awfully hard the tropics are on paper—and electronics, and metal, and pianos, and cars, and skin, and marriages. Especially when we don't have windows and doors to even try to shut out the weather. I'm plowing through files to see what can be tossed. The tropical mustiness of many of the books and papers gives off a pretty intense odor. Ty is doing the same with the bookshelves. I've already sorted through all kinds of wild poetry books.

"Can we get rid of these pink triangle Christmas lights? Please, Mom?" The lights are wrapped around the posts of the shelves.

"That's fine, hon. Just put them over there to donate. Somebody might want them."

But I can't part with most of the books. We may be the largest lending library on the island. *The Making of the African Dream, Don't Stop the Carnival,* a vintage Sunset *How to Build,* the classic *Foxfire How to Homestead.* Is that what the gals used to build this place? Perfect.

As I'm sorting, a guest jogs in through the open front doorway. It's Mauve. She has been running. She's was wearing a mauve-and-white-trimmed jogging suit (this is back in the day when people wore jogging suits). She's panting and sweaty. "Hey, Corky," she says, "sorry to interrupt you working, but I think there's a goat leg on the front lawn."

"Huh?" I say, thinking I haven't heard right. "What's a goat leg?"

"You know, the leg of a goat. I'm pretty sure there's one on your grass."

Off she goes to shower, completely unfazed. Ty and I decide goat legs take precedence over musty folders and books and go to investigate. And there it is, a small, cloven-hoofed leg of a goat, all by its lonesome self on the lawn.

My Western mind needs to explain things and hasn't yet learned the benefits of shrugging them off. I chalk it up to the goat farm across the valley and Samson, the all-muscle beagle-ish mutt from up the road. I hear he belongs to some snowbirds, but he's been hanging around La Finca since we arrived. I try calling them and their summer caretaker. No answer from either. Truth is, Samson is pretty sweet, not at all like a goat killer. He's clearly devoted to Phoebe as well, the skinny old black dog that Gail threw in with the deal, claiming that, like the antique iron ice crusher, Phoebe is part of the place. She doesn't seem fazed by much, like who comes in and out.

Over time Samson becomes our official watchdog and guards the place with a dedicated vigilance. I start to pay attention to how attentive he is. He has a different bark for arrivals: strangers, probably guests, get one bark; strangers with unknown or bad vibes get another; a horse wandering by, a totally different bark. When we come home from the beach or errands in town, no bark, just full-tilt body wag, where he curves his whole torso back and forth with joy. It's clear this little guy is adopting us.

I call the neighbors with a final warning. If he is becoming ours, that's fine. We're happy to adopt Samson. We'll feed him and care for him. But in my book that means having him fixed as well. Enough of these odd chihuahua-mix puppies everywhere. There's no response to my call, so off we go to the Humane Society on the other side of town, about ten miles away, to get Samson neutered.

A few days later I get a call, but it's not the neighbors. It's the animal shelter. Bad news. "Oh, God! What?" I shudder, fearing the worst.

"Samson is gone," the woman on the phone explains.

"Oh, God!" I feel terrible. I should never have presumed to take another person's dog in.

"No, it's not that. He didn't die. He's just not here," the woman says. "Everything went fine yesterday and they let him out into the yard with the other dogs. Today, no Samson. There is a small hole in the fence. Maybe he just dug out under. But he's gone."

I still feel terrible, but it's not like I killed him. And at least now if Samson is off on new adventures he won't be making puppies along the way. We will miss him. In just a few weeks he had become part of the place. There's a hole here now. Just like in the fence.

Life goes on. We are preoccupied with all the work there is to do and all the waves to play in before we have to head home. But other forces are at play too, what I always call La Finca's magic. Ty, a logical soul, doesn't like it when I use the word "magic" to describe phenomena, people, or places. But this place has some kind of power: It can bring out interesting behavior, at the very least, in people and critters alike. Whatever you call it, some strong magnetic pull kicks in.

The next morning I hear the kids screaming outside. I rush out and find Samson sauntering onto the deck all cocky, like *l'empereur* himself. Apparently he hasn't missed his testicles as much as he's missed us, or the place.

Our month is over. It's time to go back to Vashon, our other island, and our pre-finca life. I will hand the keys over to Bruce and Louise, who'll be taking care of this powerful place, this fledgling business and its amazing guests. They arrive a week before that to get oriented.

The morning we leave, as I'm making sure they're feeling ready to take over, Louise tells me how she'd dreamed about me the night before.

"That's sweet," I say, distracted by my last-minute running around to see what we've forgotten to pack.

"Yeah, I was practicing voodoo. On you. I had this little doll—of you—and I was sticking pins in her. Isn't that funny? Did you know I was a witch?"

"No, actually, I didn't know that." I don't have much time to worry about it. I have a plane to catch, and kids to wrangle.

Bruce and Louise don't last six months. They want a TV, among other things. They want less litter on the roads. After six months on the job, they want out.

I have to find new caretakers immediately, and Craigslist doesn't even exist at this time. Email barely does. Can you imagine? I have to ask around and around . . . and around, until I am dizzy from the pressure of finding someone good. Sure, lots of folks are interested. Words like "tropical," "island," "handmade houses," "undeveloped white sand beaches," and "wild horses" get their attention and seem to have a magic

LA FINCA CARIBE corporate hiring GUIDELINES:

always ask hiree about witchcraft

lure. It is almost scary to see how fast they jump at the chance, knowing so little about the place—did I see a pattern here? With them, and me? The problem was how to find folks adventurous enough to want the job yet responsible enough to love my darling finca as though it were their own.

Bruce calls up, I think feeling a little guilty about their early departure. "Hey," he says, "don't worry. We have some other friends here on Vashon who'd be much better suited to your place. Really. I think it could work."

Becky and Matt, our next caretaking couple, are totally sweet young people. Ahhhh, good, this feels better. No passive-aggressive pinpricking tendencies. Matt is a fireman and Becky's a bartender. Perfect. How could we be so lucky? They last at least a few months longer than the first couple before they break up. But no problem. Becky will stay on alone. This is her idea, and I don't really have a choice.

She tends our little Tree House Bar, still more a workbench/project area, but it faces west and catches the last glimpse of pink-blue twilight behind the banana grove. It's not a real, public, or legal bar—more like a club. But guests love it, and her. She makes a drink of the day, a rum punch with fresh fruit, and invites everyone in for family-style sunset cocktails. Trouble is, during the day she paints over anything that reminds her of Matt.

"What happened to that big sun mural we did in April? Am I imagining things? Didn't we paint it on my last trip down? I loved that big sun. And also the wall by the laundry area?"

"Oh, yeah, I had to erase all of those. Too many memories." Becky lasts another six months.

Note to self: Those managing La Finca love to paint. More things will be painted, repainted, or overpainted than I could ever have imagined.

I'm thinking this is what folks meant when they warned me about the difficulties of managing remotely. I sure as heck am not going to admit to any of them how much of a pain it is to find, train, manage, and keep the caretakers. Or anything else.

La Finca Caribe

Like me, our guests try to capture this place.

7.

At the Helm

Those first couple of years are like any long-distance relationship: La Finca and I get along great as we get to know each other. Our family comes as often as we can handle the long flight and rack up enough miles to get tickets. On a good year that amounts to winter and spring breaks, a month every summer, and Christmas vacation. Our visits are short and sweet, dedicated to enjoying ourselves more than anything else. David and I aren't sure enough of ourselves to make major changes around the place, just basics like putting in hot water, a septic system, a pool, replacing ladders with stairs, adding a railing here and there—oh, and hurricane straps for the main house roof. We complete walls around a few bathrooms and add color. Any wood, even plain old ply-wood, is rare in the Caribbean, so it has a charm that we might not appreciate as much in the States. I'm okay with leaving much of the place in its natural wood state, but I paint a "rug"—a large compass rose covering the main lobby/living area. "Wow, that's cool," the guests *oohh* and *aahh*. "How'd you know where the true directions pointed?"

I didn't. "Just sort of guessed."

Like any new love, I like La Finca to look her best. I see how well she responds to love and care. Like brushing a sweetheart's hair or polishing her nails, I paint her shutters, window sills, trim, and old street signs. Heck, I even paint a huge formerly white upholstered couch we inherited from a photo shoot. Swirly orange flowers help to hide its dingy self.

Years later, even the flowers show their age, so dear Jim and David, a stylish couple from Seattle who come down to manage, paint the couch a tasteful brown to go with a neutral earth-toned theme they applied to the manager's cabin. Trouble is, we don't do tasteful, or earth tones, at La Finca. Luckily I get to paint the couch red before long, because even brown gets dirty in the tropics.

During our early years here, there's only one store that "specializes" in paint: a classic Vieques neighborhood hardware colmado. You get whatever they have and learn quickly to be happy for small favors. "Hey, guys! I found a store that sells paint! And they have some in stock!"

"Good! What color did you end up choosing?"

"The two they had."

"But Mom, I thought you wanted green."

"Don't worry, we can mix them."

"But one's oil-based, the other one is latex." *No te preocupes.*

"Don't worry about that either. Let's see what happens. And they didn't have any white stain, but can't we just mix a bunch of water in it and pretend?"

The first color we ever added to the place was called "Shaman blue." It was the only deep blue—what I think of as classic Latin, like Frida's house—offered. It seemed perfect for the main house. Of course, kids being kids, mine offer to help if there's some level of danger and risk involved. Me being me, I let them. "Perfect. You guys can do the upstairs window trim. That means you have to walk on the sloped tin roof. There are places where it might be a little rusty. Be careful!"

It's perfect because it sounds more dangerous than it is. My kids are delighted because I don't usually let anyone go up on the roof. I'm delighted because it will add a lot to the house—and no one will be able to see the quality of the paint job except from afar.

"Xing, honey. You and I can find something to paint down here."

It's hot, of course. After a while Tyler decides it's time for a Popsicle break and delivers them to our various workstations. We are working away when I hear Gus come downstairs.

"Mom," he says. He sounds funny. More than sheepish, sort of scared. His eyes are bigger than usual.

"What's the matter, sweetheart?"

Holding his blue paintbrush in one hand and his half-eaten Popsicle in the other, he opens his mouth and points to it. He looks worried.

Tyler comes barreling down the stairs, yelling, "Oh, God! Mom—did you see it? Is Gus gonna die?"

Xing stands on her tippy toes to see inside his mouth.

"Oh, Jesus!" I say when I see it. The inside of his mouth is totally painted Shaman blue.

"I goofed up, Mom," he says. "I was taking turns. I'd paint, then take a lick of my Popsicle, then paint, back and forth. I thought I was licking my Popsicle!"

I have no other adult there to help with knowledge or a plan of action. Do I wash with water?—it is water-based, right? Please, God, let it be water-based. "Ty, go check the can. Make sure it says 'Wash with water.'"

And it does—he's going to live. Do I drive to the emergency room first? Are they even open?

We've been to the little hospital enough times to envision the circus this will cause. There was the time Xing was stung by the seventeen-foot Portuguese man-of-war. She thought someone had dropped a purple plastic sparkly purse in the foamy tideline. Instantly the jellyfish wrapped its long, sticky, burning tentacles around her little body. The small hospital on the island was able to help with that. Then there was Ty's daylong excursion to Culebra with an early caretaker to bodysurf. He'd patronizingly assured me that he'd take good care of both Ty and his friend Tony. The boys hated to be babied, but still, in typical mom fashion the last words out of my mouth were "Be sure to use your sunscreen." I won't try to describe the burns. They ranged from second- to third-degree. It was too much for the emergency crew on Vieques, and they sent us to a burn unit in San Juan.

Before that there was Gus and the crazy local rash, pica pica. He and I thought we'd check out the nature trails made by another caretaker, a naturalist from the States who figured guests would enjoy having walking paths through the jungle. Sounded cool to equally naive me. I'd always heard we should stay out of the woods. But, hey, if these guys built a trail, we were game. Gus came back with a rash over half of his body. The doctor said it was the worst case he'd ever seen. By now they knew me and the kids.

MORNING CHORES

WAKE UP with very first birds for the quietest, sweetest time the place has to offer: sunrise from the porch swing. CATCH BREATH, find your feet, steady yourself for the day. Then, rather quickly:

Clean overnight lizard poop from counters. Brush works better than sponge. Learn to distinguish from dreaded mice droppings.

LAUNDRY — Hang, take down, fold... endless cycle.

POOL — check for iguana guano before swimmers dive in.

Rake rubber leaves, careful for sleeping tarantulas underneath.

DETOX showers of unclaimed shampoo etc. etc.

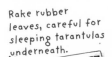

STUDY CALENDAR, like Sudoku game. Who's coming, going? Rooms ready?

SWEEP, inside and out... or, heck...will anyone even notice?

So now, the paint. What should I do? Pausing for a minute, it dawns on me that even with the four-hour difference I could call our health clinic at home. They know our family, and they'll be able to help. And they do: Wash with water. Follow with lemon Popsicle.

Because David isn't around all the time, I do—and get away with—things most wives or business partners can't, from making on-the-fly guest policy decisions to developing my own preventative maintenance program. Unlike the early caretakers, I also play the part of handyman. I learn new uses for duct tape (it can sort of melt into a permanent adhesion). I start wearing a carpenter's apron from the Home Depot in San Juan, with a roll of duct tape in one pocket and my staple gun in the other.

I don't know what's funnier, thinking of myself as handy or having a predetermined palette. Guests always comment on my color palette. I think they assume that, my having been a creative director, I give painted floor rugs and murals a great deal of thought. I don't. I use what I have in the cupboard or add to it. Anything beats another hot trip into town, especially since there's a good chance the store will be closed for the long lunch break or a holiday you've never heard of. The lack of availability and choice helps keep things simple and unprecious. That simplicity, coupled with the local (or is it Latin?) culture, is the key to the creative freedom La Finca grants me.

It's the same with groceries. You cook what you have. Recipes don't have much bearing. You buy what the store has that's fresh—or close to it, or if you recognize it. Then you quickly cook what you get before it spoils. A fridge is no guaranteed safe house here. They lose their seals, they leak, they drip. Leftovers get lost in them even easier than at home. They get hidden behind the pineapple that Room 1 left (too good to throw out). We'll toss that conch salad, but this cheese is good. And look! They must have found ripe tomatoes.

Generally we keep our things in our own fridge when someone checks in, but kids, or guests, get confused. No one worries too much about things. Our guests are notoriously easygoing.

la finca front porch

That sweet obliging property, dear finca of mine. It got by with pretty minimal care and sometimes downright iffy "management" from either side: us at home, and our folks there. Our caretakers could hardly be called managers, and I was too new to it all to be a very confident leader. David, a natural boss, was busy minding the store back in Seattle, and we couldn't change that. Merwin Creative was our mother lode: It paid the bills and rightfully took priority. I didn't yet know Vieques's weather patterns, plant life, many neighbors, or local customs. Besides, I was awfully busy with the kids and the nearly forty employees back at home. If things were okay at La Finca, that was just fine. That was good enough for me.

Now I see that we weren't so much at the helm as we were at the end of a long-distance tether. Not sure who, if anyone, was in control. It's all a bit of a blur, like a painting where smudges make things hard to recognize but indicate movement. There was a lot of that, set to a soundtrack of Jimmy Buffett and Buena Vista Social Club. Lovely up-tempo, toe-tapping music with a good beat—that didn't stop. Islanders had tried to understand the notorious ladies of New Dawn. Now it was the crazy folks up that windy road into Pilón, at La Finca.

Happy Traveling

"We don't make money, baby. We make miles." David is proud to explain this to me and anyone else baffled at our being able to afford the airfare from SEA to SJU several times a year. In our line of work, expenses are high. In those early days of the loyalty program concept, the airlines were generous. When David pays for a $300,000 Compaq print job with a frequent-flier credit card, we get the miles, and the client reimburses us a month later. Traveling gets a whole lot cheaper that way. David very quickly develops an awesome plan for racking up frequent-flier miles, big time. In addition to flying himself and our crew all over the globe for video shoots, he's basically paying for everything it takes to run our entire business on a frequent-flier program credit card.

Back in the day, things were just easier. Before 9/11, before crowded flights and security lines, we were rolling in miles and savvy about family traveling. My three little ducklings and me, we had it down.

Step One: We always booked the red-eye leaving Seattle at 10 p.m. Back then, I don't know anything better than Benadryl to help us all sleep. And, okay, I might have a gin and tonic too. Don't get me wrong, we were a health-conscious family: the tofu and spinach kind, with minimal sugar, junk food, and such. For colds, it was hot water with lemon and honey; but for long, time-zone-changing flights, we took Benadryl.

Step Two: We would take our seats, all the while keeping an eye on those empty rows in the back. Back then, there were empty seats.

The kids and I still laugh as we remember the classic, quintessential flight down to Vieques. They were still seated together in one wide-bodied center row with me, and we were all watching the movie, *National Lampoon's Vacation*. Clark Griswold was taking his family on vacation to Wally World. I thought I was going to cry I was laughing so hard. All of us were. But it wasn't that the movie was so funny. It was life, and the fact that David was up in first class. Even the flight attendant thought it was funny.

Teary-eyed and loud—that's the way we laughed. Was he anything like Clark Griswold? Or are most dads the same guy? How much of it is funny? How much is tragic? And in the end—what's the difference?

Step Three: The moment the doors closed, the kids would leap up and jettison themselves to an empty five-seat row, where they lay claim to their new territory with pillows and blankets, leaving me with four extra seats to stretch out. I was usually asleep before we reached cruising altitude.

We had a good couple of years of this sweet and easy travel, our highly functional modus operandi, before the kids started pushing into their teens, wanting videogames, in-flight movies, and sodas. Sweet and easy doesn't last forever, so you love it while you can.

As the new millennium looms, we scoff at the fearful folks stocking their survivalist pantry shelves. Instead of freaking out about Y2K, we're planning another major event, one that combines a New Year's party with our lifelong dream of bareboat chartering in the British Virgins. We'll go with a few friends, celebrate the new century at La Finca, then sail away. David orders a very large bottle of French champagne to be flown in for the occasion.

"Yep, a bottle the size of our daughter seems about right, considering the importance of the occasion," David explains, always good at justifying the extravagances. I'm equally good at questioning the expense. "Okay, Virginia," is his standard comeback when I do, referring to my exceedingly frugal Depression-era mother. That's usually enough to squelch me, but not my doubts.

Me, David, the kids. We're riding high, living the dream, or dreaming a life. My mother asks me fairly frequently if it all isn't just a bit much. I pretend I don't know what she means. There's also a Buddhist saying that the trouble with chasing dreams is that you can wake up.

Saw this cute guy at the beach

Neighbors stop by to check out the new pool

Not fake news. Real ukulele. Real beetle.

After days of trying...finally Gus makes direct contact.

Glad it was me and not guests that found what the kids left in a yogurt tub on the kitchen counter.

We've named this guy Little Buddy. He pops his head out of the sink and starts to chirp every evening like clockwork when the Buena Vista Social Club comes on...He lives down there!

Our new office assistant is really fast on the keyboard.

The Losing End

It's October, a few months before the forecasted end of the world—Y2K, when we will prove all those naysayers wrong—and David and I are at a restaurant on one of those weekly date nights David is so adamant about us having. It's bright. Japanese restaurants are often overlit, and that night is no exception. Bright, cold, clean surfaces, a typical small table for two. After ordering sushi, he tells me he needs to leave. Not for a shoot, not for a week. Not for his annual ski trip to Whistler or his annual jazz fest trip, not for his birthday golf weekend. No, this time it's me. The kids. Our life. Our home. Dreams. Photo albums. Parent-teacher conferences. Everything.

HUSBAND LEAVES WIFE OVER SUSHI. More wasabi, please. Anything to make sure I'm still breathing. That this is real. David is right there, two feet away from me. But I know he is gone. I might have been able to reach across the table and touch him. But it isn't the real him. This is the new one. Had I seen him coming? This is a 3D model, a poseur standing in for the real one. The David I married and have loved for almost twenty years is gone.

Being told your mate is going to leave you is not the same as being told you have cancer. I don't worry I'm going to die. I'm just not sure I want to live, or, if so, how I'm going to. Umpteen-plus years later, just writing this makes me pause, and look out the window and get real quiet.

Suddenly, in a Japanese flash-photo moment, the life I've built, the only one I know, the one I'm halfway through living, is broken, dangling, and will never, ever be the same. Not for me or the kids. Not for David either, although he isn't really my top

concern right then. I just need to figure out how to walk out of the restaurant, and then figure out how to breathe, and how to live.

To be fair—as fair as one can be about these sorts of things—David is pretty sweet about it. He explains how he is sure he'll want to come back. "I love you too much, honey. I respect you—so before I do anything weird, I have to move out, at least for a while." The man I consider my soul mate and the one true love of my life is apparently serious about moving out, of our home, off the island, into the city, away from our family. None of this makes any sense.

David has only recently started taking medication after suffering for years from undiagnosed clinical depression. "The meds are taking care of my mood, Corks," he tries to explain. "But they are sort of taking away other parts of me—my own motivation and direction. I'm not sure I know who I am anymore. I have to move out, off the island, and into the city. I have to figure out who I am."

Consequently, I do too. I am handed a new sad self for the millennium. It takes me most of the new century's first year to learn how to function in the world—how to be single, in my early forties, and the mother of three teens. Even walking seems hard. I watch my feet hit the sidewalk and wonder if others will notice that I don't really know how to walk anymore. I go through the motions. I fake it until, slowly, slowly, my feet and I begin to relearn how to be in the world.

I continue to live on Vashon with the kids, still working part time with David at our booming business in town. With my more-than-flexible work schedule and loads of frequent-flier miles, I escape to La Finca with the kids on school vacations, or with a pal for girlfriend rejuvenation, as often as I can. The frequent escapes help the healing process.

Although it dawns on me every now and again that it's going to be hard running the place on my own, I throw any concerns onto my "things to worry about later" pile. The finca has always been my baby. I'll manage this too.

I suspect that before long, when the kids are off to college and life, I'll be down there all the time. I'll be the lady innkeeper. Gail did it on her own. I will too.

David is a generous soul. He is happy to let me have La Finca, and he offers to buy me out of our business; the production company/creative team has always been his. We are about to start mediation and get officially divorced, formalizing this casual divvying up of our lives. This is what folks mean by "moving on." It feels like that. Things are starting to flow and work again. Xing has a starring role in a community musical. Gus is the ninth-grade prince at homecoming. Tyler is delighted to be able to play rugby—escaping a lot of the home-front chaos—at an amazing boarding school a few hours away on Vancouver Island. We are all beginning to be okay—in fact, really fine.

A year later David and I begin to be on friendly terms. He offers to help me choose a new car. I'm partial to the used Jetta wagon. "Listen," he says, "I care about your safety, and that of the kids." The look in his eyes is nothing but loving; it's just a new kind of love. "I think you should get the new Saab wagon." When I wrestle with the extra cost, he takes me aside for some classic David advice. "Hey, Corks, when are you going to accept the fact that you're a wealthy woman?"

I know at that moment, standing there in the Carter VW & Saab dealership parking lot—and have always known—that I will never feel wealthy or know how to recognize our prosperity. I understand we are extremely fortunate, but wealthy? Never. My response to David's advice, though, is, as usual, to cave. I buy the new Saab. I pretend to accept that I am "a wealthy woman." But I don't have to keep that act up very long.

David comes over to the island a couple of weeks later "to talk." That's weird. He pretty much avoids Vashon and our family memories at all costs. He arrives looking awkward and confused.

He's spent the weekend at his CPA brother's house going over some numbers—what he calls oddities—that David has found in the books. As soon as he begins to describe in detail how odd these oddities are, it's like the time-slowed sensation of a car accident. I can see that we are sliding, tumbling down into an ugly rabbit hole that, like Alice's, doesn't make sense. Stranger still, we've apparently been falling for some time without knowing it.

For years David had grown our production company into something almost larger than life. "The fastest-growing communications team in the Northwest." Big, smart, fun—a wild ride at an amazing time and place. Seattle was on a roll. Grunge was playing, the world was discovering software and coffee, and they were all taking off. We were there to help launch it on film and video. David had taken our homespun creative duo from an Anchorage split-level basement with a playpen for Tyler to the newly remodeled top floor of a historic building on Capitol Hill, with three edit bays and forty-five employees—many of whom were now asking for an espresso machine in the lunchroom and preferred catered Christmas dinners to my annual home-cooked leg of lamb. The world was changing much faster than I could.

But after twenty years at it, and looking age fifty straight in the face, David wasn't focused on Merwin Creative anymore. Just my luck to have my husband's midlife crisis collide head-on with the economic crash of 2000. What we couldn't begin to know at the time was that we were on the cutting edge, first tier front row of the dot-com bust. No wonder our largest client, Compaq, had suddenly stopped hiring us to travel the globe for extravagant film shoots and marketing campaigns. When all those little start-ups they were making computers for began folding, the last thing they needed was another server.

Boom. The sound of big, big waves crashing. Being among the first to fall, we had no context, we didn't know what was happening. No one else was going broke—yet. But that too would change. What David discovered is that our general manager, the smart guy we'd hired to be oh so much smarter than we were at running a business, had been using our monthly revolving line of credit as a regular business loan. David would never have done that. Even I knew you didn't confuse your regular business loan and its low interest rates with your revolving line of credit and its astronomical interest rates. Years earlier David had explained that we'd only use the credit line when we knew money was coming in.

Guess our general manager didn't take that class in his MBA program. He had borrowed $750,000 on our line of credit, hoping something would come around. On top of that, he'd run up $300,000 on our American Express bill. This wasn't *Wolf of Wall Street* decadence; these weren't parties with senators and call girls. This was day-to-day stuff: massive printing jobs, airline tickets, office supplies, and salaries, salaries, salaries. Bottom line: We weren't just wiped out flat, like the red, bleeding tide of dot-commers would be soon; David and I, two regular, middle-class folks, were personally $1 million in debt. Feel free to read that line again. I always do. And I always think I must have got it wrong.

Finca? What finca? My little island paradise evaporated, as if Vieques had broken free from its mooring and drifted to another distant sea. The finca was quite suddenly the last thing on my mind.

Immediately we break our own golden rule and have to lay off the staff. Brutal. We had never laid off anyone for lack of work, and we don't have a clue what is happening with the business, or much else. I go back to work full time.

I discover the healing nature of country and western music. I learn every word of Iris DeMent's "Easy's Gettin' Harder Every Day." I learn to belt it out as I walk through the gray wet, down the hill to the ferry to Seattle. By the time I'm walking the mile through downtown to the remodeled loft office we can no longer pay for, I'm writing my own songs. And I am truly belting them out. I have nothing left to lose. I learn what that means. I am off to work every day with my ex. And not just to work, but work together to try and save this sinking ship.

David and I are not technically divorced. Lawyers make it clear that couples owning a failing business aren't allowed to divorce until things are financially resolved. That will take a couple of years (in fact, it took three long years). We live in a land of hellish limbo. Tyler comes back from his private Canadian prep school for his junior year. After school he bags groceries at Thriftway to help out. Gus is in middle school. He still wants to go to the expensive snowboard camp from our previous life. Snowboarding has become his salvation. He starts making pies to sell at Vashon's annual Strawberry Festival to pay his way. Xing sells her harvest of miniature pumpkins at the farmer's market. It all helps.

Yes, indeed. Be careful what you wish for. But what about being mindful of what you're afraid of? Ever notice how the things we fear the most are just what comes along to bite us? Years earlier, back in Anchorage, Alaska, at age twenty-eight, married for four months and pregnant, I was afraid—just very sure—that David would leave me when I was in my early forties. "I'll be left to raise the kids as a single mom!" I cried to my good friend Margie over tacos at Mexico in Alaska (odd name, great food). She was a little older and had been through a divorce and single-mom childrearing.

"Don't worry," she counseled. "Worst case, if you're right and David leaves you and the kids, you'll still come out okay, because you'll be a mom and that's not a bad thing. That's the good thing. The best thing—ever."

It wasn't like I spent our years together worrying about it. I'm not a big worrier, and we were

MY OWN RED RIVER VALLEY
(sing as close to that tune
as will fit, with as much twang
as you can muster in the
Seattle gray)

i've lost more than i could ever count
now — lost it all; let it all wash away
but i'm standing tall in the sunshine,
and to god, i daily do pray

it's not a prayer asking for more, now.
it's not a prayer to atone for my sins.
it's a prayer of thanks for my loved ones
— there's nothing above friends and kin

when i was young i held life in my pocket
strolled around with good luck by my side,
but these days for reasons i can't fathom,
all my luck and good times seem to hide

step by step it's starting to come back
bit by bit, all is returned
not to the old, but a new way, of livin'
— to the old i will never return

cards are dealt, and played round the table,
some hands win, while others will bluff,
just be sure you're up for the game now;
cause sometimes the playin' gets rough

the answers are all out before us.
it's the questions that are harder to find,
grandma said it takes love and forgiveness
— it's that, and a whole lotta time

lost in new weeds.

very much in love for most of our seventeen years together. I just sort of saw the ending right from the beginning. How much credence do you give to fearful premonitions? To this day, I don't know if it was based on something David did or said. His father's legacy? Or my own, perhaps: Since I was raised by a single mom, that picture of reality was all that I knew firsthand. Men left. Moms stayed.

So that happened. Sort of. It's not like David abandoned us, but the net result is pretty much the same in the end.

Bottom line, at forty-three (which felt so old then) I'm single, with three teens, no job, no business, no resources. Not a whole lot to hang my hat on apart from the kids, who are teens and thus not so interested in hanging out with me. We sell what we can at a giant garage sale. I still regret getting rid of those Ninja Turtle action figures and my painted postcard desk. But the house we are moving into is too tiny for the storage of sentiment.

Ty is off to fish in Alaska for the summer before starting college in the fall. Gus, Xing, and I gather what we can and move to Seattle. It will be okay. Friends joke about my "witness protection plan." LO-freakin'-L, as in not. My standard response is that we've lost everything but our health and senses of humor. Ha ha. Sometimes I add, "Oh, and my mind. I lost that too."

I don't know if it's a good thing or fair, or if it makes me feel any better, but the banker who kept lending to us loses his job, and our general manager does own up—kind of. He turns to me as he's leaving the office with his things and says, "I will take this remorse with me to my grave." That doesn't make me feel any better, but it does help me realize it's all real, not a dream I will wake up from.

Now I wonder if he does still carry that remorse with him. Before I learned how to block his page, his name and smiling face used to come up on Facebook as someone I should "like." For many hard years I'd drift off to a fantasy about asking him for some help with college, just to make things easier on the kids. Then I realized, with the whole reference to the grave thing, that he might be planning to leave them a little something in his will. One can only hope.

Somehow the hard years roll and fade away, and the kids make it through college—and it's all somehow okay.

empty.

the page
my heart
my life

the blue sky in its emptiness
seems to smother us all

Solo

Yep, life began at forty. Just like Mom always said it did. At forty I woke up, took stock of where I was and where I wanted to be. I had all the kids I wanted. I had found La Finca, and things had fallen into place. And then they all fell away. If life had begun, it ended three years later. Or maybe Buddha was right. If all life is suffering, then I was really living.

My forties were very much what I had feared almost twenty years earlier, and a little worse: unemployed, underloved, and overwhelmed—in Seattle, a city that, other than the search for work, made little sense for me.

"You're not a city girl, Corcho." I don't need Rocio to tell me that anymore. I know it, but there I sit, with little more than the knowledge I was right at twenty-eight that David would leave me, and right later about getting this cool funky place called La Finca Caribe, with its handmade houses on a beautiful piece of land, on a little island no one has ever heard of. Problem is, I don't have the money to maintain the place, the frequent-flier miles to visit, or the mental space to deal with it. It doesn't help that we've only owned it for three years. We are still newbies to it and to Vieques, the culture, the climate, all of it. And now I'm going to have to run it singlehandedly. From afar.

The first thing I need is more money, in a big way. Three years before, Hurricane Georges hit and left a pretty big mess. (The Powers That Be somewhere finally decided that home-wrecking storms could be named after men.) Georges took down some of our largest trees, wiped out parts of our buildings, and knocked out our landline—our primary means of doing business—for a couple of months. As a relatively new student of Puerto Rican utilities and bureaucratic ways, I was appalled at the phone company's lack of responsiveness.

I want answers. I want things to make sense. I also need to make money. To make matters worse, FEMA decides against giving us any financial help. We don't qualify because our business in Seattle has made too much money. Business in both places has slowed down so much that neither is generating money. There I sit in Seattle—3,768 miles and a million light-years away—helplessly watching the finca from my distracted mind's eye, unable to pay for basic repairs. I manage to exist on Buddhist self-help books, the abundance of free furniture folks leave on the sidewalk, and the fact that unemployment keeps being extended for anyone in my profession and region—apparently the worst combo in the nation.

A well-to-do former Microsoft client and friend partners with me to open a small gelato and postcard shop in downtown Fremont, our arty neighborhood village. For years at Merwin Creative, when the going got tough with overly demanding clients, I'd laughingly said, "Wouldn't it be more fun to hand someone an ice cream for a living?"

It is, in fact, a lot more fun. Within a couple of months of opening, I have regular customers whom I love. Channeling Juliette Binoche from *Chocolat*, I know what flavor

they need by the way they walk in. I don't make a dime—hourly it amounts to less than minimum wage—but the work gives me a focus as I search and network for a creative director position between scoops. My career, my whole life, feels like the ice cream scoop scraping across the bottom of an almost empty tub of gelato, trying to come up with enough to scoop.

And the hits just keep on coming.

Unfortunately the one thing we haven't lost is a large, looming personal loan from a wealthy friend, Louie, back when Merwin Creative started to topple. David is more than comfortable asking Louie for this short-term loan because he knows large checks are due any day from Microsoft and Compaq, and he is absolutely right. The checks do arrive. What he doesn't know, however, is that any incoming money goes to the bank, not to us. That's when I learn the meaning of a secured loan.

Louie is a real character. He retired at thirty from Silicon Valley. He's originally from China, and his family was prosperous there even before he amassed his own wealth in the States. As crazy as it sounds, back in those high-rolling days we feel okay asking him to lend us $100,000. The contract on a paper napkin seems, even to me, a tad too casual. But we don't treat the loan casually. For the next couple of years, every month without fail, David and I scrape together—between the separated two of us—a monthly loan payment with interest, as agreed.

Somehow the news of the loan finds its way to Louie's dad. He is as surprised to learn about the loan as we are to hear about him and his increasing involvement, regardless of our regular monthly payments. Every few months, then weeks, Louie asks if we can pay the loan in full. There is no way we can do that, as we have already lost our home and all of our assets.

Around this time I'm starting to date Gene, a dear Japanese American man, a fun guy, and we laugh a lot together. We have just sat down at a cafe bar in a small town in the outback of eastern Washington. In that moment, all is well. Somehow over coffee we start talking about the difference between Japanese and Chinese surnames.

"It's simple," I, the self-proclaimed Asian scholar, explain. "It's all about the syllables. One, straight up, means Chinese. Japanese names have a minimum of two, and more commonly four—like you, Takahashi."

"Nope, sorry, white girl," Gene says, laughing. "You're wrong there. I worked for a Chinese guy with a two-syllable name: Jon Son. Sounds just like Johnson."

"That is so weird! I guess you're right. My friend—remember the one I told you we had to borrow all the money from? He has the last name of Johnson too, and he's Chinese, but I always thought that name was from a marriage generations back."

The color change on Gene's face gives me pause.

"What?" he says. "I mean, who? Who do you owe that hundred thousand to?"

When I explain all of it to Gene, he gets very serious. "Corky, I've worked for this guy. I know him and what he does. Do you know what the Tong is?"

I know then that I'm in a whole new big kind of trouble: tôNG,täNG / *noun* / a Chinese association or secret society in the US, frequently associated with underworld criminal activity.

Stop, already! We've lost it all, and now I'm on the hook to the flippin' Tong for a hundred thousand dollars? Scenes from *Married to the Mob* and *My Cousin Vinny* start rolling before my eyes. I'm a regular person—how can this be? I can't tell if my life's a tragedy or comedy, or maybe a farce? Do I even dare tell the kids?

Then I remember that their favorite movie is *The Usual Suspects*. They'd love it. Kobayashi. Gangsta-everything is all the rage. This would make me cool in their eyes. Whatever.

Soon after my conversation with Gene, Louie comes to me with the option he and his father have worked up: La Finca. The one thing I have somehow saved from the creditors. They saw it as a crazy place with no value, something they didn't want to deal with. Well, Louie knows differently. He has been there.

"We need you to sell La Finca, Corks. Sorry. There's nothing I can do."

In all fairness to Louie, I'm sure he feels his father's pressure as much as I do. But there you have it. Even though we've never missed a payment, and even though each one includes the going money market interest rate, Dad and his accountant don't like the idea of an unsecured loan being out there. La Finca will have to go up for sale.

The truth is, I'm so used to losing it all that I just put it on the proverbial list of things you must let go. Poof. If I touch it, it will die. Who needs attachment? This whole material ownership thing is *soooo* overrated.

Soon thereafter, La Finca Caribe is officially on the market. I grew up with Janis Joplin preaching, "Freedom's just another word for nothing left to lose." I've always been down with that. But now I am about to lose the last thing I have. A friend asks if I've given any thought to who I might have been in a past life to warrant all this. "Like a Nazi, maybe?" she says, laughing. Friends can say the darndest things.

LOVE THE FINCA?
OWNERSHIP IS A BEAUTIFUL THING

dear guests and finca lovers –have you ever considered being a part of it?

the finca is looking for investors or partners, to help us manage and market our little piece of heaven –even from afar, like we do, we are flexible, and interested in creative ideas of co-ownership; exploring ideas from offering a second home escape, to furthering the retreat aspect of the finca, or looking down the road at developing the world's coolest retirement community, feel free to share these offers and ideas with your friends & cohorts back home.

"there's a hammock with your name on it, waiting for you, at the finca"

for information:
corky merwin
innkeeper
email: lafinca@merwincreative.com

la finca caribe
rustic villa & cottages
po box 1332 vieques island, pr 00765
(787) 741-0495
http://www.lafinca.com

la finca caribe

Folks start looking at the finca for its business potential. They want to know what the place makes so they can figure out what they can afford to put into it, to make it normal. Real walls, real doors, dishwashers, clothes dryers—how much will it cost to make it airtight so we can get AC in the bedrooms? Real rebar on the windows? Maybe even pave the driveway?

Around this time a bomb used in navy training kills David Sanes Rodríguez, a Viequense civilian who worked for the navy. In sad, angry response, anti-navy protests from the island community heated up in earnest.

I know enough of the history to be outraged about how the US Navy expropriated two-thirds of the island in the 1940s for its training. Entire towns were emptied, families evicted from their homes with no plan, no alternative housing provided. The navy takeover has always sounded horrible but somewhat abstract, until one day when I offer lunch to a cleaning lady and her sixty-five-year-old mother, Maria, who is helping her. The three of us sit down at a table on a shady end of the deck.

Maria describes their plight calmly and matter-of-factly in Spanish. "My parents worked for the sugar mill," she says. "It owned our home, everyone's homes. Then all of a sudden we were forced out." That had happened nearly fifty years ago.

"I was fourteen," she continues. "Without warning they came and made us move. We had to live off the land, with only palm fronds to shelter us. We lived like animals, all my brothers and sisters, on the side of the hill. We looked for anything we could find to eat. I was pregnant and married at fifteen. But at least our family didn't get broken up. At least we didn't have to move to Saint Croix. We all got to stay on Vieques."

I am in awe of Maria, still filled with humor, energy, and apparently forgiveness. She gets back to making beds. I get over feeling too sorry for myself. Or try to.

We want the navy out too. We offer discounted stays to visiting protest dignitaries who are coming in to strategize. We are more than sympathetic to *la lucha*, the cause, the fight. To be honest, I don't know if I really believe that a small band of locals on a tiny Puerto Rican island has a lizard's chance of getting the US military to do anything, much less leave a strategic fifty-year-old navy training base. But, heck, go for it.

So just as La Finca goes on the market, Vieques becomes a symbol of Puerto Rican solidarity and US oppression. The support for La Isla Nena is clear wherever you go in San Juan. I love it. And I love NPR too, but not the way they are starting to make the protests sound. No one is "rioting in the streets" here. There are large urban demonstrations in San Juan, in sympathy, but they are peaceful. And here the demonstrations at García Gate are peaceful too, small because everything on Vieques is small, consisting of friends and community leaders. No one is getting hurt, no one is even afraid of getting hurt. But the US media shows scenes in San Juan, and cancellations start coming in. Large groups can't risk it; business dries up.

And if few folks want to rent a room on a bombed-out, riotous island, fewer still want to buy the place. I nudge the realtor to market it more assertively. He rarely returns

someday i'll gain perspective...
maybe

my calls. I try to explain this to Louie, who in turn explains it to his father and the dreadful accountant.

I can't figure out why the realtor isn't more motivated. "Come on! No matter what we sell it for, you'll make your commission and I'll get to pay off the Tong!" Mysteriously, there's no response. I know this guy. He is sort of an island friend, such as they are. I've been to parties at his sweet villa. His partner once brought me a bottle of rare tequila from Mexico for my birthday. So what's up with lack of response? How do I make it sound convincing to Louie, reassure him that I really am trying? (Years later all was revealed. My realtor had had other priorities. He'd just gotten on the board of directors of one of Vieques's most important nonprofits, and he was very busy embezzling a million dollars from them. No wonder.)

Comparatively, the sale of my finca is pretty small potatoes. But not to Louie, who takes me to lunch. He is sort of squirmy. I'm not worried, because I know, straight up, about turnips and blood. There is nothing left to squeeze out of me. The finca isn't selling.

"I'm sorry," I say. "I have no way to pay you, Louie. We. You. Your dad and the accountant. We will all just have to wait."

"Actually, they've found something else," he says, and squirms again. "They found your mom's house. In Sonoma. You can borrow against that."

If Mom's little house was a Monopoly property, I'm guessing it'd be a red, like Illinois. Middle of the humble road, nothing ostentatious. And she doesn't own three of that color—or anything else.

This house is really all she has in the world. I see it turned over. For the first time I now get the whole "mortgaged" thing.

"Hi, Mom." (Mom, who could never ever understand our lifestyle or La Finca, who always thought David was living way beyond his means. The mother who, like so many, turned out to be right about so much.). "Look, I don't really know how to ask you this . . . There's this guy we know. He's a friend we owe money to, but his dad—his dad is a member of the Tong. Have you ever heard of the Tong?"

Mom does what moms do for their kids. She mortgages her home and lends me money to pay off the loan. Boom! Finally I am out from between that rock and hard, scary Tong place.

Afterward I don't have lunch with Louie as often, but that's fine. Monthly payments now go to Mom. Within a few months we sell Merwin Creative for something like fifty cents on the dollar. At least as important as the little bit we make out of the deal is our ability to officially divorce. After three years of working together, separated and waiting, it's done. I'm officially free. Or just single.

"What a tangle of threads with untraceable origins I discovered in myself in that period."

—Elena Ferrante

11.

Aftermath

Good news, bad news. This beautiful palm-tree-and-mango-studded, be-careful-what-you-wish-for piece of paradise now officially belongs to me. Me alone. Well, me and the kids, but three teens who, at that time, are more interested in Puerto Rico's cheap rum—and lower drinking age—don't help much. Yep, this is all mine now. This and all the headaches. Managing the managers, taking care of the caretakers. Here I am. To be more precise, sadly, there I'm not.

We've always managed the finca remotely, with frequent visits to check in, complete projects, or provide vacation relief for the managers. Now I'm an owner without the financial means to get there for any reason. I can't give La Finca the time and attention it sorely needs and deserves, so more than ever I must rely on the managers. When they don't like all that comes with managing, I change the job title to "innkeeper." When the concept of keeping an inn seems like too much, I try "caretaker," as in "Just take care of the place": *Puhlllease take good care of my baby.* But even that descriptor doesn't fit sometimes. Maybe giving them more responsibility would be helpful, so I try "manager" again. We are running in circles.

From how to hang the linens to whether to roll or stack clean towels, one caretaking team will only work under certain rules and conditions, and the next is adamant about the opposite. And they care about these details like I would never, ever have imagined. They can't all be crazy; it must be me. But the truth is, I can't seem to connect well with most of the folks I hire. At the office, in the real world, I could. But not so much here, where everyone is chasing their own personal key-lime-pie-in-the-sky version of paradise. Even when I think I'm connecting with them, it turns out I'm not.

It's okay that every new manager knows a surefire way to decorate the rooms, or beat the power of the tropical sun. I've learned the odds are slim to none that it'll work — but I also learn to let them learn this on their own.

So, they don't listen to me. I now know not to take it, or much else, personally. (That lesson took a tad longer.)

Note to self: For every lesson you learn, there's an infinite number of sublessons circling around it that you gotta learn as well.

The ones who seem so solid really aren't. The ones who are solid don't last.

The kids and I come down once a year, if we're lucky, to provide vacation relief for the managers. That way we avoid overlapping with them for more than a day. I can't understand why the kids and I feel such hostility when we arrive. Or am I just imagining the passive-aggressive chill in the air? As much as I seek out staff to share the place with, sharing it ends up ranging from emotionally challenging to darn near impossible, harder for them than for me.

Looking back, I can see it's because I knew intrinsically, down to the bone, that the place was mine. Not in a possessive way—it's just reality. I lucked out; I'm the lady who got the finca. It was actually easy and rewarding for me to share it with folks. That's what hospitality is all about. Most of the managers who came and went over the years fell in love with the place pretty seriously. It took me years to figure out that when the kids and I arrived, our presence was a larger-than-life, heartbreaking bummer, a reality they didn't want to deal with, staring them in the face screaming, "This place that you know and love and care for every day isn't really yours. It's hers!"

Over the years, different caretaking staffers have contacted me to apologize for their behavior while they were at La Finca. One even called me from Japan, where he was teaching. "Hey, Corky, it's Rob. Remember I used to caretake La Finca for you with John? Like ten years ago? I just wanted to let you know I'm sorry for the way we treated you sometimes, way back then. We were just so young and stoned most of the time. We didn't know what we were doing."

I remember. In the middle of my financial meltdown I had come down to deal with Hurricane Georges damage, and I did an almost unimaginable thing—I spent thirty-five dollars on a new dress. A sweet, sexy sundress, midnight blue with flowers, a short, sheer dress with spaghetti straps. I don't shop much now, and back then I didn't shop at all. An equally rare thing for me then was feeling sexy and cute, so this dress meant a lot. The day I'm leaving, and doing my laundry, I notice that despite its sheerness it still hasn't dried.

"Hey, Rob. I have to leave now, and I still have one dress on the line. It's a new one—a treat I gave myself. Will you do me a huge favor? Will you just put it in a bag by itself, and stick it on a shelf in your cabin?"

"Huh?" Rob looks up from painting his rum bottle collection. (Sounds weird, but they were beautiful, and clearly therapeutic for him. He'd painted dozens by the time I returned that fall.)

"Rob, I really need your help. I know John has too much on his mind, so I need you to focus."

I'm thinking about the concept of focusing, and in my mind's eye I can't help but see the bong that was on the coffee table when I arrived. ("Oh yeah, we had a party the other night.") "Look, I'll be back at Christmas. That's only three weeks from now. Can you promise you'll just stash this somewhere when it's dry, and keep it safe for me? I really love this dress. I know it sounds dumb, but I never buy new clothes for myself." As usual, I go on too long to make sure that he got it. I know, considering the bong, it might be asking a lot.

But he doesn't think so. "Sure. No worries."

As scheduled, I return three weeks later. "Hey, Rob," I say, "where'd you end up putting my dress?"

"What dress?"

Was he stoned when I'd asked him the first time? Or was he stoned now? He hadn't lost it. He hadn't ever touched the dress. Too bad it's not still flapping in the breeze. Whatever. Add it to the list of losses.

The next couple I hired to manage, Steve and Tina, weren't stoners. They were newly-weds, arriving with a just-married idealism and energy, and uber-responsible. Even better: uber-confident. So much so that they just did things. They didn't ask. Maybe they told me later. Like when they gave away the antique cuatro, a Puerto Rican fiddle-like guitar, to a "really neat" couple from the main island who apparently really liked it. The same confidence let them feel okay about taking Phoebe, our old camp dog, who'd been with us since we got the place. All she'd ever known was La Finca. When they moved away to New Mexico, so did she. No asking. They just took her, assuming they could care for her better. Need I go on?

Then there was the couple a few years later that thought it was okay to adopt a dog while they lived at La Finca. Not one of the island's chihuahua mixes, but a Samoyed malamute—very large, with lots of long hair. Not okay, and not a good idea in our climate. Bad for the furniture (back in those early days managers let dogs sleep on our lobby couches, despite my protestations), and really bad for the pool, where the dog

So many birds, still unknown to me, sing from equally unfamiliar vine-covered trees. I can't see them, but five different calls surround me as I write. It's magic.

There's something like 125 species of birds on this island. How many will I get to see and know? I know it's their home. I know we're the visitors. The guests.

Faraway roosters and dogs from neighboring hills add to the mix; even silent lizards make remarkably loud crunching noises in the grass and leaves.

I always think it's something bigger and scarier — an iguana, a rat, or the almost mythical wild boar, the javelina — but it always turns out to be just a lizard.

swam and played every day to cool off. I wanted to throttle them. Even my adolescent kids knew better.

Don't get me wrong. These guys had it tough in the early years. Their pay was low, the conditions funky. Business was slow, at best erratic, so there weren't funds for many improvements. Back in the day, there wasn't even a bathroom in the manager's cabin—they had to walk next door to the main house. Same for the showers. Our caretakers had to share the shower house with guests, and if we were booked, our solar hot water system was so primitive that often there wasn't enough hot water for everyone. The finca trucks (we've had a long lineage of classics over the years) seemed to self-destruct within just a few years of use, so the windows didn't roll down, tailgates didn't open.

Nothing was easy or normal. The internet and phone were both iffier than they are now. Either one could go out for days or weeks at a time. I couldn't believe our reviews rarely reflected the funk; something about the magic of the place hid it, I guess. Few folks seemed to notice or mind the dogs or bongs, or the casual approach to housecleaning.

When the evening dishes are done and the kids are off doing their own thing—Scrabble or Risk, before the days of videogames—I take to my favorite nighttime hammock, the day's big payoff. My ultimate getaway (every innkeeper needs one within reach) is on the upstairs deck of the main house. Up there, I'm high enough to be away from any light or noise. If there are guests or anyone else around, I don't know it. I can swing in the quiet, balmy blackness that covers me like a silky air blanket, studded with soft sparkles. The night sky, so different from home, sways back and forth in sync with me and the hammock. Even Orion lies down on his side here. Sometimes I see Scorpio—stars we don't see at home. They are my true friends, leaving me only for the time it takes for the occasional cloud to pass.

Since I was young, I've measured my happiness and good fortune in seeing shooting stars, full moons, and birds of prey. If I am lucky enough to see a hawk, it means

this place has known me

NO LIFEGUARD
ON DUTY

morning tea

two before the others
book or artwork or
list of things to do

floors + the tables
siblings + children
gypsy kings. laughter.
rice + beans

sometimes rain   always breezes
          always

today i knew
yoga stretch
east indian
career as a

something: an omen, an undefined milestone, a sign that somehow that I am on the right path. More hawks, and it means that much more—of whatever you choose to call these markers. It's as if the stars or the great powers of the universe somehow keep score for me. Here in my hammock, I can see any number of stars; it's usually just a matter of lying still and letting them come to me.

After a year on the market La Finca has still not sold. Louie has been paid off, but now that we are divorced, David rightfully wants his half of the money we have in the property. I try everything I can think of to sell it. I watch a movie about auctioning off an inn—I try that. I look to friends, past guests. Who wants in on a timeshare owner-ship arrangement? Cohousing? How about an alternative retirement community?

I try to give it up but can't figure out what that means, what it would look like. If I could, I would, but who is there to pass this torch to? No one wants La Finca. No one has heard of Vieques, and no one seems interested in hearing about it.

And then the phone rings. It's Anne, a dear old family friend.

"I just heard from Jane that you're officially divorced," she says. "Congratulations—if that's what one says. I've actually been sort of waiting for this news because, well, you know how much I love La Finca."

Anne is lifetime best pals with my oldest sister. She came into my life when I was three and they were both fourteen. We come from the same hometown, Petaluma, and her parents and my mom hung out in the same North Bay Beat enclave. I played with her younger sister, Molly. When I was six, the older kids married me off to her brother Billy, also six. I remember losing the wedding ring—that sparkly, sexy ten-cent thing—on our first day of wedded bliss. I wasn't used to wearing bling and wanted to find it badly. But their family's sprawling ramshackle farm property had lots of nooks and crannies, and it could have been anywhere. Eventually I gave up, sad to lose it but relieved not to have to worry about being married. *Everything in due course. No need to rush things.*

Anne had first come to La Finca years earlier, soon after we bought it. I knew she loved it and felt the same connection to Sonoma County in the early 1960s as I did, some kind of geocultural DNA we shared. Anne had moved to New York and done well in the restaurant world—really well. The two of us have always shared deep bonds; for one thing, we were both entrepreneurial worker-bee types. Despite her large-scale suc-cess and my own less-than-stellar track record, we recognized each other's "self-made businesswoman" essence. She is recognized for knowing how to run a great restaurant, how to serve a great meal, how to make the Clintons or the Rolling Stones or any num-ber of celebs feel comfortable. But I always admired most is that, despite the success and recognition, Anne's downhomed-ness. She knows how to work hard, recycle, and repurpose everything possible.

"My lawyer said I couldn't help you when you were married. Too complicated. But now, my friend, any chance you'd want a new finca partner?"

Clink, clunk. The sweet sound of things falling into place.

Lost forever,
but never forgotten.
The dress I wore
twice...

12.

Meanwhile, Back at La Finca

Anne's partnership helps tremendously. I think it is about five years after buying La Finca and two years after putting it up for sale when, voilà—I'm no longer alone in the decision-making; I have someone to bounce ideas off of. Then, coincidentally, miraculously, after ten years of ongoing community protests, the navy pulls out. Who could have possibly imagined this would happen—and on George W's watch, no less? The US Navy leaves Vieques, relinquishing their sixty-year control over two-thirds of the island. Most of their massive share of land goes to the US Fish and Wildlife Service. Cynical locals laugh that control of the island has only shifted from blue uniforms to green—or whatever color rangers wear.

Suddenly we own the only eco-inn on the island with the largest "wildlife refuge" in the Caribbean. Vieques is in the limelight. A travel writer for the *New York Times* notices one of our handmade signs on a telephone pole, finds us, and falls in love. Who cares that the article refers to me as "some dotcomer from Seattle" and the current manager hasn't thought to call to let me know the writer was on the property? No prob. We get a photo and several columns in the *NY* freakin' *Times*.

Business picks up. We put a bathroom and shower in the manager's cabin. Things start to improve. I begin to know myself as a single person, and I like the me I am becoming. I find a little freelance creative work back in Seattle so I can afford at least an occasional glass of wine with friends and new Nikes for the kids.

I start to date again. And if the question doesn't come up on the first date, it certainly does by the third.

Guy: What was that you just said—about you *owning* an *inn*?

Me: Yeah. It's sort of hard to explain. I mean it's not like a real, normal B&B or anything. It's just this funky place in Puerto Rico.

Guy [confused or incredulous]: Where?

Me: You know, Puerto Rico. In the Caribbean.

Guy: [*Quiet.*]

(Regardless of how adventurous they claim to be in the match.com profiles—and no matter which pronunciation I use, *Ca-rib-bean* or *Carib-be-an*—these aging, supposedly wild and crazy guys always look confused.)

Guy: You don't mean *the* Caribbean?

Me: Yep, that's right!

New to the dating scene, I think of La Finca as an asset adding to my total package, maybe a second marriage dowry, my own cowrie shells or goats sweetening the deal. It doesn't take me long to figure out that instead it's a giant red flag that screams, *Run, buddy, run! She's weird!*

I can't tell if they imagine I'm a swashbuckling lady pirate or the crazy lady from *Wide Sargasso Sea,* but they rather quickly ask for the check, and as always I pay my share.

Over the course of my so-called fabulous forties, a couple of guys I am seeing brave it and come down to see the place they've heard so much about. One sheepishly admits after he gets there that he doesn't really like water.

"Okay. No beach—and no pool time," I say. "That's cool. There's always stuff to get done around here."

Then he cops to not being much of a handyman or feeling real comfortable using power tools. *Hmm,* I wonder, *how's that going to work?* Except for being in water and fixing things, there's not all that much else to do down here.

Then there is the handy type of guy who knows all too well what repairs are needed. He takes one look around at the endless array of work projects, staring at him longingly, like hungry children and is totally overwhelmed.

"Are these decks up to code? Or, are there building codes here? I mean—is it safe to have hammocks like that? Don't you need railings?"

"You know, it's weird," I say. "I don't think there are codes here. Not like at home. It sounds odd, I know. But everything is different here. I'm not sure. You've got to understand, it's not just me. Down here, no one knows for sure."

But they don't understand. And they don't stay long. Changing innkeepers-caretakers-managers and boyfriends, I learn that no matter what they all say, no one lasts.

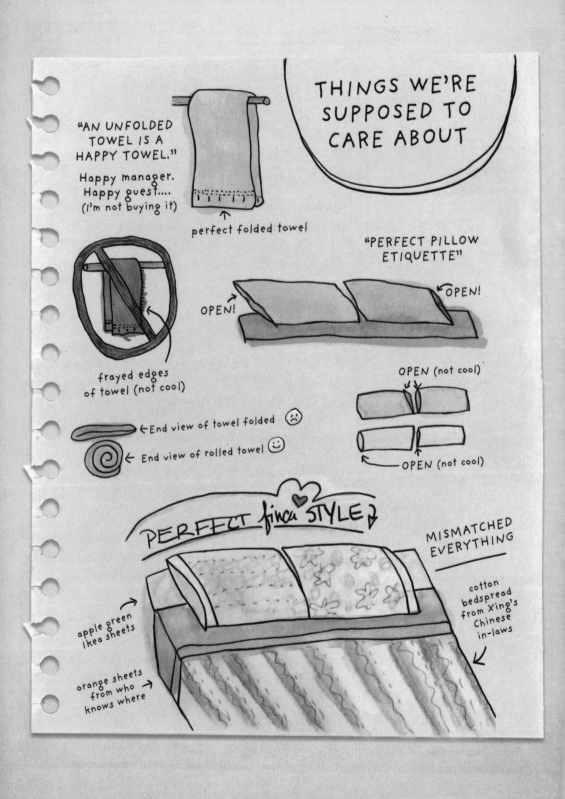

13.

On-the-Job Life Lessons

La Finca has always been my teacher. Lots of other things, too—my healing place, my escape, an amusement park, a child-care facility, my family and friends' employment opportunity—but above all, my teacher. She is usually a gentle, passive, free-school type of teacher, the kind who sits back and lets you learn at your own pace. Sometimes, though, if I'm not paying attention, she takes the wheel or slams me up to the wall to make sure I got it. I've learned it's best to do my homework and be prepared before that happens. La Finca can be a little tough.

I want to understand Vieques and Puerto Rico better, so I set out to do my research. I ask a lot of questions. What's a territory? How's that different from a colony? What's a protectorate? How do senators from Puerto Rico work without the ability to vote? What's this Three Kings' Day holiday all about? Why is the island's largest hardware store closed for twelve days? Why do we need a lawyer to get something notarized? What's Spanish law based on? How did we get a car inspection sticker without getting the car inspected? Where does this government tax go? Who oversees the ferries? Why do the nails bend? Why do our new appliances break so quickly? Why do folks stop their cars in the middle of the road to talk to neighbors? And why do the folks behind them not mind? Why are twenty-five cars lined up at the gas station, and why doesn't the gas station take credit cards? Why is a horse skull left on the front yard in the middle of the night? Why is there so much AC on in the hospital that patients and staff have to wear warm jackets? Why do quotes for the same project (legal, engineering, construction, etc.) range from $500 to $20,000? Why wasn't the purchase of our land ever recorded? Why are our laundry baskets always missing?

HOW TO CATCH &
release A TARANTULA

1. find hole

2. find dried grass
                stalk

QUIETLY drop
grass into hole

3.   pretend to
                be a bug
                who has
                fallen into
                hole.

4.   when you feel gentle
      tug, slowly draw grass
                back out.

5.   as you see his
      legs grasped
      onto your line
      pull him out
      long enough to
      say hi and snap
      a pic.
      et voilà!

Why did I find a cookie sheet and cutting board under the bed in Room 1? Why does that one guy show up with girlfriends to hang out by the pool once a year in the middle of the night? Why is so little local produce available? And on and on.

Nothing makes sense. Logic isn't always apparent here. Smart locals are infinitely more accepting than their northern comrades about taking things in stride and letting unsolved mysteries stay unsolved. Many of the explanations turn out to be related, and not just in our imagination. The appliances do break and the nails do bend, because Puerto Rico is a colony and has no real control of its destiny. US corporations take advantage of that and send the worst-rated, poorest tools, or models that are no longer sold.

It's not Puerto Rico's fault that the quality of so much of the merchandise and food is so low. Locals learn not to expect much. From funding to policy, so much is out of their control, a certain Buddhist-like "Que será, será" approach to life sets in. Over time one learns the futility in asking why (*por qué*). It gets you nowhere, just leaves you more confused and frustrated. Over time you reach the next level and rise above the frustration. And you learn various lessons along the way.

When we first bought La Finca, I wanted to be outside as much as possible. At night, when my time was finally free, I would lie down on the little hill (what had been a horse pasture and had become a lawn) and watch the night sky. Sure, there were little antholes, but the ants didn't seem to come out at night. I would stretch out, sigh, and finally relax, alone with my stars.

A pilot from Puerto Rico who was staying with us at the time asked, "Would you and your kids like to learn how to catch tarantulas?"

Of course, the kids were literally jumping up and down, chomping at the bit. The more potentially dangerous or weird anything was, the better. "Yeah!" they screamed.

"I guess you can take that as a yes, but what makes you think about tarantulas right now?" I asked him.

He smiled and motioned casually outside to the rubber tree. "Because you have so very many of them. In all those holes."

Maybe he read the shock on my face. "Did you not know that?"

"*Tarantulas* live in all of those hundreds of holes? That almost perforate the grass in every direction? You aren't serious."

He reassured me there was nothing to worry about, that they are very timid and only come out at night. *Right where I've been lying down to watch the stars AT NIGHT?!* Even the kids stood wide-eyed and incredulous for a minute before they took off running to be the first to catch a real, live tarantula. Their new favorite tutor and hero followed them.

Note to self: I will learn a lot from my guests, and more from the locals.

Knowing how to catch a tarantula turns out to be one of my most valuable and secret innkeeper assets. It's one of the few things I'm reliably pretty good at. Families-in-the-know arrive having heard from their friends about our (in fact, the pilot's) surefire knotted-dried-grass fly-fishing catch-and-release technique. It makes for great photos of their kids coaxing the small, shy monsters out of their dens for a quick hello. Kids and sometimes even their parents squeal with triumphant delight. And I learn to relax with the stars from the hammock.

I read the classic authors: García Márquez, Vargas Llosa, Borges. From them I find that living with mystery and the supernatural can be reality in Latin America. I learn that things actually do disappear here. In fact, it's so common that it's attributed to "porch fairies." There is often little perceived value to the item that goes missing. It can be a sheet, a laundry basket, a small wrench. Poof!—gone.

Sometimes though, it does have value. Like with the "Terrible Unsolved Mystery of the Beer and All Else."

One Christmas a family rents our big six-bedroom main house for a private family reunion. These are our easiest guests. The manager's cabin and office is right next door if they need anything or just want to chat. They take the place over and have a ball: hammocks, decks, and views in every direction.

The father, our main contact for the group, checks in a few hours before the others. He asks if we can hold off on our "rules of the ranch" orientation until his wife gets in. That's always a problem because the place is filled with idiosyncrasies—from "Why not?" to "Yes, do worry about the iguana you might find in the pool," from porch fairies to recycling. All stuff they are going to need to know, but his wife doesn't get in until late, so no prob. We're flex. They are from a town in the States that is so very hip, it's famous for it. And he is a writer. So no worries anticipated. We plan to meet up in the morning. These guys are very chill, and they've been great so far.

First thing the next morning, however, the writer's wife comes up while I'm hanging laundry. From how well she is dressed, even on waking, it's clear she is not our average guest. I haven't seen pompoms on black heeled mules in a long time (for straight men and others who may not know what all that means, let's just say they are fancy slippers), and never at La Finca.

Oh, the things we've learned from...

UNIVERSIDAD de **la finca**

The tiny white balls we find in the nooks and crannies of the lofts aren't scattered breath mints or miniature mothballs, they're lizard eggs. (I only find out when I knock one off the bunk bed, and rather than land, or bounce, it HATCHES! and runs across the floor.)

At check-out the nicest young hipsters can threaten to go online with the photos they've taken of the lizard poop on the tops of the mosquito nets — and ask for a $500 discount due to the stress of worrying about "health hazards."

Light switches can work for your wipers.

Boundaries need to be drawn and maintained. When and how to listen to sorrows without getting sucked in.

The mind-boggling range of family dynamics, values, and behavior you witness from reunions can teach you a lot.

Guests really feel okay about not having paper napkins if you provide them with their own napkin ring for their own cubby for the week.

Weather has little to do with if a guest has a great time or not. They bring their trip with them... it's packed in their bags like karma.

Thrift stores have the best, softest, 100% linens. I learn to mix and match the colors and prints from varying eras.

Daily clean, recycled beach towels work great instead of paper towels, & kids take to simpler living much easier than their folks do.

Your friends with enough money to be adventurous and spontaneous often aren't, and those without money are...

Combining friends and family in the same reunion can be a tough or interesting combo.

Puerto Rico won independence from Spain, becoming an autonomous government on July 17, 1898, but somehow lost their new independence within the first month, when Spain ceded it to the US as part of the Spanish—American War.

Turns out Yoga groups are second only to weddings as most demanding guests (don't worry, I love yoga, I do yoga, some of my best friends... and all that). I'm just sayin'. Very exacting.

To have a lot of dental and medical done in Puerto Rico at a fraction of the cost, with doctors and nurses trained in the US.

Things that look great painted intense, bright colors in the tropics usually look ridiculous back home.

Painting Casa Grande dark blue actually makes the rooms hotter inside. Who knew that the sun would soak into the blue, and make south-facing walls hot to the touch all afternoon? It does warm the towels on the wall rack.

Puerto Ricans will look you in the eye, smile, and say "Buenos Dias" in elevators, on buses, etcetera, but if you try that at home everybody thinks you're crazy.

You don't have to worry when you find out the purchase of your property, 15 years prior, was never recorded, and that's totally okay, in fact common. The paperwork is literally just sitting on a desk, or in a basket, waiting to be recorded.

Great, fresh, local produce is growing all around you, even if it's not in the stores.

They all think you're crazy... pretty much no matter what.

Back home, after seven years of being single, I'm learning different things. Like who I am on my own, and how to be okay with it.

It's actually really cool the locals stop and talk to each other in the road, holding up traffic for a minute or two... It means that you get to do it too, when you start to make your own local friends.

A friend fighting breast cancer, looking at her final months on the planet, can be overjoyed just to pick ripe mangoes.

be very interesting if you aren't

And, that it's very important to be careful what you wish for, and how it ca

learning the difference

between what I see & what I want to see...

above all, learning to let go

"Can you tell me how this whole communal kitchen thing works?" she asks, obviously not happy. "I mean, can we just have our own fridge?"

Okay. For me, first things first: I say good morning, but that doesn't get a reaction. So I go on: "Oh, you don't have to worry about that." I try to sound reassuring. "You guys have rented the whole house. The kitchen is yours, both fridges."

"No, we don't have the whole house," she says. "Someone is sharing it with us, because someone is drinking our beer."

I try to be subtle when I glance over at their kids, late teens/early twenty-somethings doing the "hang at the kitchen table thing" just inside.

"Last night after we went to bed, someone drank two of our Blue Moons. And it wasn't one of us." The woman is clearly pissed—at me especially—even though I didn't drink her dang beer. I'm the lady who owns the weird frat-house-hippy-commune kind of place that her husband clearly chose, and that's reason enough.

Damn porch fairies. They rarely ever come inside, and they never, ever open the fridge. I'm sort of speechless, and she picks up on that.

"Can you ask around? Like, you know, the people in the other houses?" She gestures, sort of dismissively, to the casita just below us.

"Oh, it wouldn't be them. I know that much. He's a district attorney from Pensacola, and he and his family have been here for a week. And up in yellow house, that's the dean of Swarthmore College. She and her family come every year. We know them well. They wouldn't take your beer. And in the cabaña, that guy is in his nineties. He can't walk that far, and his wife, she doesn't drink beer—"

"Well, then, *who did?* I mean, the place has no doors, so I guess anyone can just walk in, anytime?"

Now, gentle reader, and potential or verified finca guest, I ask you: Do I confess to something I sure as heck would never do, or point the finger at the likely young culprits who are absentmindedly pouring milk onto their Cap'n Crunch? Having raised three teens by this time, I am pretty sure I know who took the lousy beer, but I stay mute on that front. I'm thinking it's way too late to try and explain about porch fairies. This is the sort of dilemma that budding innkeepers may not imagine when they are dreaming up their *Fantasy Island* career path.

"I have no idea," I finally say. "But I am so sorry it happened. I really can't explain it because we haven't had any sort of problem—you know, thievery, burglary, anything—in years. And never from the fridge! How weird!"

"Whatever," she says, and shrugs. She starts to walk away, back through the beaded curtain that separates their kitchen from my laundry space.

"I can sit down and go over everything with your group, once they're all up," I call out, still trying to show her that we do run a tight ship, appearances notwithstanding.

But, like her husband, she isn't interested. "I think we're good," she says. "We travel a lot. We can figure it all out."

Bummer. That's always when things fall apart, I think, as I fold the last pillowcase and head straight back to my cabin.

Not fifteen minutes later the soft-spoken husband appears in my office/living room. "We have a problem," he says. He looks grim. "I can't find my briefcase."

I will spare you the gut-wrenching and really heartbreaking details of the next hour and a half as he and I and his now furious and incredulous wife, his kids, his arriving siblings, and other guests look for the briefcase. Because it is sad. He's terribly sad. And we are all sad that something inexplicable and bad has happened. But it is also just weird.

A man in his fifties, smart enough to write books and travel a lot, goes to bed upstairs and leaves his briefcase downstairs in the open-air living room lobby of a place he's never been before? And what's that—it has $2,500 worth of cash in it?

He tries to explain that this was my doing because we said we prefer not to take credit cards. And what else? His new Mac Air computer was in the briefcase? With the latest manuscript of his book? Are you kidding me? Oh! And his passport? Not to mention the 500 euros on top of the $2,500? This is a nightmare.

I call the police. Even they scratch their heads on this one. I am sure they are more than familiar with porch fairies and probably equally experienced in real theft. But when they see a place with no doors and no rebar over the windows, that makes them roll their eyes. And if the place isn't weird enough, guests here go to bed leaving their valuables five feet from the open door—all night? Gringos locos. And they're right. I'm sort of thinking the same thing.

"The wild thing," I say, "is we basically have no problem up here. We haven't had anything taken from the main house in over ten years, at least. We're too far out of the way, I guess. It's not like we have much of value up here or get many people just passing by."

The police are even more baffled; I can see it in their eyes.

"How does it happen that the one time in ten years someone comes by to steal something, there's something so valuable to steal?" the young officer asks me.

"I have no idea," I say. "But is the missing beer any kind of clue?"

"No. Just makes it all the more mysterious," he says as I walk him and his partner out to the gate. "We'll let you know if we get anything on this, but don't hold your breath. The worst part is, of course if a bad guy did stroll in on this one lucky night, that's really bad for you, for La Finca. Now you'll be on their map."

Ugh! I shudder. I love being off the grid and off the radar.

No matter who stole the stuff or what happened to it, now I'm mad at the guest for making things feel creepy and vulnerable for us all. We rarely lock the doors we have. But I feel for our guest too. He's clearly distraught. Every so often he offers up an impressive "There's got to be a lesson in this somewhere"—an attitude of unattachment. Heck, I even feel for the wife in the fancy slippers, because it's not healthy to be that angry. She fumes at him for leaving the bag downstairs. She throws dagger eyes at me. "You really should warn people that this happens."

"Actually, we do," I say. I try to explain that it's in all the reservation information and on the site, but she's not interested.

"I could meet with you guys now, if you want," I add. I know it sounds dumb, but they still don't know about the recycling, or how to use the solar showers, or the parking etiquette.

"No. That's fine. I think we know enough at this point. Besides. It's not like we lost all our money or anything. I still have another $3,000 cash in my purse."

Claro que sí. Of course you do. *Todo es muy, muy misterioso.*

The hardest part of accepting a "mystery lesson" is getting comfortable with the concept that those you call friends might steal, cheat, or mislead you. Whether it's about taking a sheet or the cost of lumber, or getting repair folks to come back to finish the job, you need to be okay with not knowing if the behavior is malicious or even conscious. This is the tough one. This one takes time.

Eventually you get there. You can continue to trust—because you'd be hosed if you didn't—but you learn to stay unattached, to the missing sheet and pretty much anything else. So instead of being hung up and demanding why, with the futile *por qué*, demonstrating classic Western attachment, one learns instead to use *porque*, which means "because." Just because. And that, my friend, is a great step toward true Viequense acceptance.

Not all mysteries remain unsolved. Some are figured out, and often the *porque* behind them is pretty humorous. Like the week of the banging pots in the main house kitchen.

One afternoon the pots and pans that have hung for years from different lengths of chain from the kitchen ceiling begin to sway. Now, that in itself is no big deal. As any finca regular knows, Casa Grande is prone to shaking. A five-year-old running across the deck can get her going. It doesn't take all that much to get the whole two-story building sort of trembly. The first time I notice it, I naturally think that the winds that blow through our open-door, open-window *cocina* have just picked up, and I ignore it.

The next afternoon around three o'clock I am in the kitchen cleaning up from lunch when the clink-clank of pot hitting pan starts up again and evolves into a gentle rhythmic banging. A good-size yoga group from Canada is staying with us, so I think they're probably on the side deck doing sun salutations, but no. I remember it's their quiet down time. Most folks are at the pool or off to the beach. It must be Samson scratching away at a flea or some such thing. That can do it too. Oddly, though, I don't see him anywhere.

By the third day, when the clinking starts up again at three in the afternoon, it feels more mysterious. Same time as the day before, and maybe the day before that. Now that's weird. Why every day around the same time? Can winds or fleas kick up on schedule? This time it isn't windy, the dogs and kids aren't around, and no one's doing sun salutations, so what is going on? I get real quiet so I can think clearly. Do I hear laughter?

"Who the heck is in Room 3?" I think I'm talking to myself, but Amy, an intern helping around the place, says, "I think that's the instructor, Shanti."

"What is she doing up there?"

I thought the place was empty, but wait! Before either of us can move forward with our Sherlock and Watson imitation, the dreadlocked group cook, Tony, saunters downstairs. Just like he had in the days before and would for days after, like clockwork at 3:30. With a lazy grin, he says, "Buenas tardes, beautiful people." Amy and I keep looking at the counters and floors to hide our smiles. Shanti comes down a little later.

Innkeepers learn to be discreet. I take the pots off their hooks and put them on shelves, where they've been kept ever since.

The wind is picking up, pushing out the day's heat, a pre-evening almost-chill in the air. A guest, a retired public defender, is here with me, quietly playing one of La Finca's guitars. How wonderful it is to not know someone but still be able to share a porch, an early evening, and favorite songs. This kind of magic is what this place is all about.

The pre-evening riotous chaos begins when all the birds and bees and bugs around come out of their nests and holes, turn over their leaves, and get going, start tuning up—are they competing? There are times when it's a symphony, when they share the stage, giving each other a moment to shine and sing. And then there's the cacophony, like now.

A good-sized bird lands in the tree next to me. He jumps from branch to branch squawking loudly and assertively. Is it a grackle? It's hard to know the birds around here. You rarely see them. They live most audibly in this persimmon dusk to just before our pale apricot dawn. They are creatures of the night. And they're loud. *Ruido.*

Recording the sounds doesn't do them justice. After a while, once the skies are truly black, the bird-bug screech-scratch-squall mellows and the natives settle into an almost-rhythmic beat that continues steadily into the night, unless a sudden shower erupts. When there's new water to sing about, the frogs go a little crazy.

14.

Bill

We meet on a blind date. A dad of one of Xing's classmates works with Bill and wants to set us up. It isn't an online sort of deal, but it might well have been. I walk into the Lock Spot, a favorite dive bar and diner among Seattle's fishermen. We are meeting for breakfast. I take one look at Bill and know, right off, that he's not my type. Nothing physical, mind you, but he's wearing a Nike baseball cap, and his clothes are high-tech athletic stuff (I'm more the wool and denim type). Besides, he already has a Bloody Mary in front of him: Apparently he has a drinking problem to boot. We'll make this short.

Then we start talking. Now it's not like it was all sudden and gushy—just the opposite. After eight years in the dating game, I am over the mushy stuff. I've fallen in love—or down rabbit holes—more times than I'm comfortable admitting. At this point, I'm pushing fifty and jaded, or maybe, just maybe, gaining some wisdom. In any case I'm certainly tired of the dating game. But still, there's something about this guy and the way he talks about his kids, their trips to Mexico, river rafting, and cooking Thanksgiving turkey together, and his recent trip to Barcelona and ensuing love affair with Spain. Bill seems completely unassuming. Talking over breakfast is easy.

After a breakfast of favorites—French toast and bacon—we walk out to a classic Seattle landmark, the Hiram Chittenden locks. We pretend to watch the fish and boats make their way through the canal to and from Lake Union out to Puget Sound. I am bundled up against a chilly April day. I am wearing my thickest ironclad thrift store Cowichan sweater and my favorite old tight black jeans. This was back before the days when they had to stretch to fit—not that it matters, of course. What matters is how comfortable I feel.

That I remember what I ate and wore, and how comfortable I was on our first date is a flag, some kind of subconscious nudge. I somehow asked my memory to sit up and pay attention: This is a day worth remembering. And it's all effortless.

It's so easy being together, in fact, that rather than playing hard to get, or any other game, Bill and I break the cardinal dating rule and go out again that night. The kids let me off the hook for our usual roast chicken Sunday dinner. Gus and Xing are in high school now and probably couldn't care less about family traditions anyway. Bill really wants to take me to a film about Billie Holiday and Frida Kahlo. A coworker has given him tickets. I've never heard of this film—and about two of my heroes, no less. I don't know if I should be dubious or really impressed.

We go off on our second date of the day. The underground film is apparently so underground that it's playing in the basement of a cafe in Ballard. Sure enough, it turns out not to be a film at all. It is a wild, rather amateur and ambitious spoken-word thing. Bill is apologetic but not mortified, like most anyone else would be. He handles it well, laughs it off, and at intermission turns to me and says, "Wanna get the hell outta here?"

Rather than losing points for a dud date, he gains with the way he handles the dud, big time. His ego is not fragile. This guy can handle a storm, I think. My life has recently been tumultuous, so I like that.

Our second real date is at an outdoors Lucinda Williams concert. Nothing goes wrong, although we're both mildly surprised and somewhat disappointed that she doesn't find us in the dive bar we escape to afterward. But who cares, I'm just happy Bill shares my love of funky neighborhood bars. Our third date is a hike and picnic on Ebey's Landing: an open farmland and beach area on Whidbey Island's western coast. The view—the gateway from Puget Sound to the Strait of Juan de Fuca—is stunning. I've never been here before, and I'm blown away by its beauty. From the bluffs, as we walk looking out over this intersection of waterways, the Olympic Mountain range seems to float on its own peninsula, balanced by the San Juans and Vancouver Island to the north.

Bill seems equally impressed by the picnic I've packed: cold lamb chops, dolmas, goat cheese, and veggies, the remaining goodies from a dinner with girlfriends the night before. What impresses me more than anything is that at the end of the long day, as we're driving home, a deep, growing sense of comfort and ease sets in. It feels okay to be me, the real me. Neither of us is faking or posturing. Here is a man who might be falling in love with me without putting me on some stupid pedestal.

Our next date is a hike on Mount Rainier—my idea and a sort of test on my part. For me, hiking is an essential skill in a man. It takes a while as we traipse along the forested path, but eventually Bill quietly lets on that he actually climbed Rainier, as in summited it, a few years back. All 14,400-plus feet of it. This guy is no braggadocio. I will have to pry his stories and accomplishments out of him.

BILL

Name: William T. Parker.

Sounds normal enough. Then you find out he has no idea if the "T" is short for Ted, or if he is in fact "T." Hmmm, not as normal as first impression

Personality: creative, quiet, kind, and comfortable

Hobbies: running, cycling, his Moto Guzzi, wooden boats

Profession: Architect

Pets: one small calico cat named Belle

Favorite Authors: Jim Harrison, Eduardo Galeano

Dislikes: anything tasteful or trendy, leftovers

"Oh, so you taught at Columbia? After you went to school there? Was that before you worked in China, helping to design medical labs with the Rockefeller Foundation?"

It's rare indeed to find other folks who have spent time in China back in the day. Like me, Bill has wandered through the old Beijing, the one with Hùtòngs and alleys, and witnessed the sea of blue Mao-suited bicyclists filling its boulevards, changing like timed tides, at their block-wide intersections. We have these weird things in common. The trails ahead, like the stories behind us, unfold, revealing more.

Driving west home, the sun is setting, filling the car with that last red-orange evening light. Tired and happy from the long day in the mountains, I put on Angélique Kidjo's first album to complete this perfect scene. The thing is, I can't listen to her without dancing. But what the heck? Bill might as well get to see another, deeper part of me: the core of me that can't help but move to music I love—not quite uncontrollably, but unselfconsciously, at least on a good day. If Bill can handle having me car-dance right next to him—if he still wants to have anything to do with me, or better yet, if he doesn't make fun of me or ask me to settle down or be more normal—this could get interesting. I've held off falling for that sweet smile of his or looking too long into his deep blue eyes. I start singing along and moving to the music. Bill just smiles, nods a bit, and taps his fingers. He has passed another test, without knowing it. It's all good. It's all real good. It feels safe, as well as fun. What would happen if I just let go with this man? Is it that safe?

Bill's two daughters, Win and Jess, both in their mid-twenties, live far away. Bill lives in a cool little house he's bought and half-remodeled (the other half just waiting in a tasteful architectural version of suspended animation). It's in a part of Seattle that's remarkably still woodsy, shaggy, down a long driveway, completely hidden from any street.

Bill may not say a lot, but his house speaks volumes. I recognize both his renegade self and sweet design sense as soon as I step inside. Later on a few honest friends openly call it a hovel, and they laugh. But I love it. It's an unusual and wonderfully comfortable combination of funk and high design. The entire kitchen still has the original 1940s linoleum, stove, and cabinets, right next to Bill's clean architectural upgrades like metal roofing for exterior siding and long rolls of bubble wrap for light diffusing and insulating shades. The whole place is essentially one big open room, like a treehouse loft.

"I have to tell you," I confess, after I run around admiring the happy mix of family treasures, Ikea, and garage sale, "I was a little nervous to see your place. Guess I was afraid that it'd be all cold and modern and ultra-tasteful, like most architects' houses. But it's not any of those! I love it!"

"Yeah, I don't really do tasteful." Bill shrugs off the compliments. "Not if I can avoid it."

So that explains it. I've been wondering what this classy, mysterious guy saw in me. I love the originality of it all, and the way he thinks. If you used the words "shabby chic," he wouldn't have a clue what you were talking about. It's clear this new guy I'm dating is not only unconventional; he also doesn't give a fig about what most people think of him, or anything else. Like his hidden house, he is a little above it all, removed, and kind of hard to figure out.

"I think you're going to love La Finca," I say.

Bill and I date for about six months before we decide to make our first trip together to Puerto Rico, Vieques, and . . . La Finca. Traveling from the West Coast, fatigue and jet lag are real, not to mention a first-timer's culture shock. It'll be easy to get over-whelmed. I decide before we arrive to give him the space and time to soak it all up.

From that perfect first vista, Bill scans the place from left to right: the family cabaña poking out above its scarlet bougainvillea, the pool nestled in the giant ginger and hi-biscus, the solar showers almost hidden by the massive rattan plant, the casita peeking out from behind the mango and bamboo, and our big blue main house looming above its front wall of bananas, palms, and lobster claw. Its front veranda turns into a wooden walkway that leads to the manager's cabin. It's almost full circle to where we stand, hot, sweaty, and tired in the shade of the monstrous rubber tree, our rolling suitcases on pause for a moment. I'm thinking, I hope he gets it—or will, eventually.

Bill is quiet. No wonder: It's a lot to take in, especially after a night without sleep. But his isn't the typical gushy love-at-first-sight reaction so many folks have walking through the gate and down to the rubber tree. Even impatient me has learned to give Bill time. He's what is called nowadays a slow processor. On top of that, words don't come easy for him. So I wait.

Throughout that first day there together, I see Bill wandering the property, taking it in in his quiet, thoughtful way. He's looking everywhere, under cabins and over roof-lines, at solar water systems and our funky cistern, checking out the potential proj-ects everywhere and my duct-taped fixes seemingly in every corner of the place. Bill's less-than-demonstrative reaction has me a little worried. Will any potential partner ever get the why and how of this place or just feel its magic?

When I've gotten settled and it's time to enjoy the evening, I find Bill sitting on the main house's swinging bench. It hangs on the same big rusty chains that it has from our first days there. The swing serves as a sort of throne to the whole finca. Not in the sense or ruling over the realm, but, rather, as a holy meditative place. It's at the end of the deck, closest to the banana grove and its large granite boulders. Below, just over the rail, are two palms and a small plumeria. At the far end another palm juts out of the hibiscus hedge that rims the deck. Between the palms, the swing looks out over my favorite view anywhere, the rolling hills of Pilón and the valley opening and spreading out to the Caribbean. I never tire of it. I never take it for granted. And despite the island's development, this view has stayed as true to my first day as the bench has.

Hard to say that the evenings are the best time on the swing, because the mornings from here catch the sunrise. But evenings too are heavenly. Like clockwork, as the sun sets over the hill just west of us, the twilight's symphony of frogs and crickets starts up. The pink-apricot popcorn clouds turn to periwinkle, and the palms and bananas become black lacy silhouettes. The palms start to rustle and the first star twinkles into place. I hand Bill a cold local beer and join him on the bench. The chains creak their acceptance, and the swing regains its rhythm. Then I see something in his face, and I know it's safe to ask. "So, whaddya think?"

The swing swings. The fronds sway. "It's spectacular," he says, then pauses for a long time. I wait. "I can't figure it out. The buildings are pretty funky. Like you said, there's no end to keeping up with the place. I've never seen duct tape, or a staple gun, used so creatively." He pats my leg and keeps swinging. "The landscape, the climate, it's all really beautiful, but this building, this crazy, out-of-anything-that-follows-code building, is spectacular."

Does it call to the architect in him? Or the renegade?

"Have you ever realized how much this house is like a big old wooden ship?" Bill says. "A little derelict maybe, but just like a wooden boat: The more love you pour into it, the more she responds. You can feel how much you love the place. Goofy duct tape and all."

MY WOODEN BOAT IS A HOUSE

In the boating world, few are crazy enough to go for wooden vessels: lifetime projects of love & toil. Similarly smitten souls relate, others just scratch their heads. But Casa Grande, like any boat worth its salt, has weathered many a blow. She's the largest in our fleet: a rambling, hand-built, six-room guesthouse, and the heart of the finca. We live on her decks, sleep in her berths, oil her wood, and scrape the rust off any hardware exposed to the moist salty air.

Like a boat, she creaks and groans, sorta bends, in a good, strong wind. When we were new to her helm, it worried us. Back then we thought we were in control and logic prevailed. We added massive, stanchion-like cables, strapping them over the roof to hold it on in a hurricane. It's worked so far. The place is still standing. Half of the stays are shot now, rusted through. Like loose rigging, their whirring sounds add to the nautical romance of Room 4 especially. One learns to turn liabilities into assets.

Casa Grande sits where the land slopes southward, and so its big deck stands high off the ground, its prow facing squarely into the trade winds, which hail from the southwest, across our midship. To harness them, slightly starboard, we hang our laundry.

If you've ever taken down sails in nasty weather, you know how scary it is when they wrap around you, tugging at you with a life of their own. Our large queen sheets can be just like that—flapping, snapping, and flying, sometimes downright horizontally, enshrouding you in faded pink or bright apple green, threatening to knock an unsuspecting crew member or housekeeper off the deck.

Many a time, I've wondered if the long scratchy fall down through the amapola hedge might be my eventual demise. One hand for the boat; one for yourself. It's a boating mantra. Don't let go.

...wooden house in the Caribbean is a rare and wonderful thing...

"WOULDN'T YOU RATHER JUST GET A LITTLE DUPLEX IN TOWN?"

Her bow is a big deck, looking out over hills that roll out to the Caribbean, and on to my favorite horizon anywhere. Turquoise meets robin's egg blue in its own clashing way, as if sea and sky are wearing colors that shouldn't go together, but somehow do. They pull it off, except of course when enormous tropical clouds take over, separating the two with varying grays and pinks, charcoal to apricot.

Off to portside lies St. Croix, showing itself as different sizes and versions depending on the day and haze. Theoretically Venezuela is out there, due south. Doubt we'll make that far in this thing, but it feels good knowing a place as foreign and exotic as that is our next-in-line neighbor.

In summer, right at dusk, the Southern Cross appears just above the neighbor's goat farm. It slips below that horizon quickly. Twilight doesn't last long in the tropics. The next thing you know it's another jet-black, star-studded night sky. A skilled sailor navigates by stars, but we just stretch out to watch them, share our salty, sandy tales, trying to chart what's coming next.

"WHY WOULD YOU WANT WOOD?"

"FIBERGLASS IS SO MUCH MORE PRACTICAL."

I've yet to find the words to explain the rationale of a boat, or the finca. What would I do all day in a little apartment without laundry to fold, a painted floor to touch up, tropical problems and Latin mysteries to solve?

After years adrift, just when I learn to single-hand the place, I meet Bill, wooden boat guy, who prefers the lines of midcentury classics to anyone or anything young and sexy. He's an architect to boot. He gets the whole finca thing. He gets me. Bill cautiously steps aboard, and we are on course, underway.

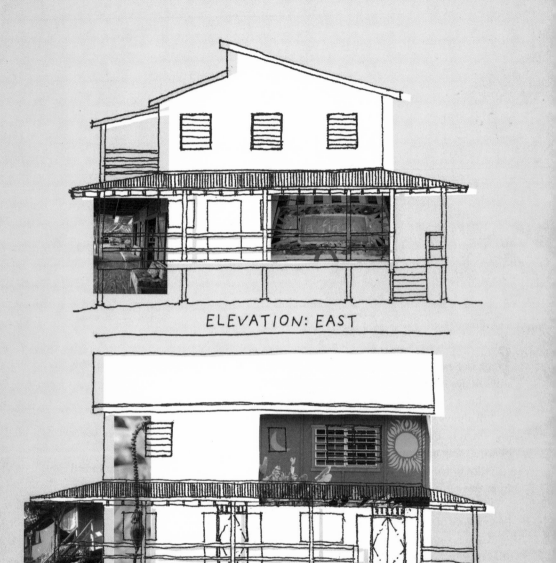

ELEVATION: EAST

ELEVATION: NORTH

Chaos of Construction

Back in Seattle, a few months later, it dawns on me that Bill might want to try his skills at designing a small house that isn't wood.

"I know of a lovely little piece of land on a small island in the Caribbean."

Bill always sees through my silliness. "I thought the place was perfect as is?"

"Oh, it is. But wouldn't it be nice to have a place we wouldn't have to worry about blowing away in a hurricane?"

"Not to mention a house we could live in whenever we get older and want to bail from this rat race—you know, like retire?" he adds.

I like the sound of that. I can't tell if it's out of his love for me, the place, or his lifelong love of drawing up plans, but Bill is on it.

Anne is on board as well. Bill, a former New Yorker, hits it off with her when we stop over in NYC to brainstorm ideas en route to La Finca for our first monthlong winter stint together. Anne, Bill, and I share a common approach and like the idea of building something that will be a solid version of the rest of La Finca. Building funk and comfort into a house from the onset is an interesting challenge. We will keep it simple. We will build it ourselves, with our kids. That's what we think.

"No. No. No!" Tito, our neighbor, is loud as he refills his glass—and Bill's—for his regular evening visit on the back deck. Tito is a Spaniard by birth, a wise world traveler, adventurer, and jack-of-all-trades. He is our best friend on the island and a contractor

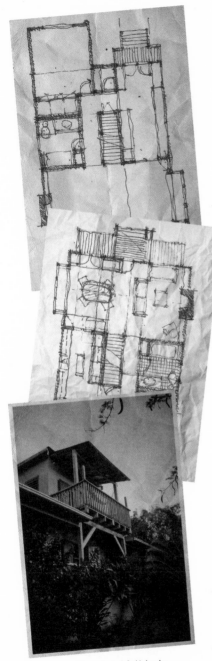

Wonder if this is anything like what Bill had in mind...

of sorts, or a retired contractor, when he's not running restaurants. Whatever. He is usually so relaxed, but about the idea of us building, he is very clear.

"You can't do that. You will make too many mistakes. You don't know enough. You'll get in trouble, either with the authorities who will hassle you for not filing the right papers or by others you have to hire, who will rip you off. Trust me!"

We do. Bill and I decide against building ourselves in favor of placing our trust in Tito. Unbeknownst to him, between Tito's barrel-chested stature and his morning and evening walks with his little dogs, we've long thought of Tito as an accidental security guard patrolling La Finca. No one is going to mess with the place as long as our neighborhood *padrino* is on guard. The cost of this casual but effective sentry duty is minimal: either a cup of strong coffee or a glass of *vino tinto*, depending on what time of day he passes by. He loves the company, so any invitation is a good excuse for him to come in and rest and tell us great stories.

We love Tito. Not just because he makes the best paella and pasta carbonara at his place, in his outdoor gypsy kitchen wagon. Not just because he invites us up to watch the World Cup, forgetting that between our numbers and his lack of furniture or space, all of us—Bill, Xing, Gus, at least a couple of other kids, and I—will all be on his bed to watch Spain beat whoever. And not just for all the rosemary plants and gardening advice he's given me over the years, or because he looks like Anthony Quinn and acts like Zorba. We love him for all this, and for being our friend. So it doesn't take another glass of wine; we are already convinced he's the guy to build our house.

With Tito hired, I'm excited that one-half of the couple I've hired to manage the place is also a carpenter/contractor. I am finally hiring real, live, experienced innkeepers, professionals! Polly and Rob are downhome honest midwesterners who have run inns and want out of Michigan, or Wisconsin, or whatever downhome honest-to-God heartland place they are from. Bill, Xing, and I get to know Polly and Rob in our week together, and we both feel comfortable and excited about all that we want to do together in this new year.

"This is going to be a great year!" Rob tells us. "I'm just sorry I didn't get down here sooner. I could have managed the crew you have on the new house project and saved you a bunch of money. But I'll still be able to watch over them."

The timing is bad, but Polly and Rob will have their hands full just getting up to speed; they don't need to supervise construction on top of everything else. Besides, Tito is on it.

Before too long, Rob emails to ask if they can remodel the manager's cabin. Seems like an odd priority. "By doing it now, we can piggyback on the other construction, the materials and tools," he says. When he senses I'm not really buying it, he goes on. "You see, Poll and I want to start a family. We need a bigger cabin. We want to put roots down."

When I explain that Bill is going to want to see a sketch before we can decide, Rob reacts almost angrily. He's put off that we are both showing a lack of trust in his professionalism. As an architect who shares drawings of his plans with people every week, Bill is more than confused by his attitude.

Before we can figure out how to proceed with the idea, Tito starts complaining about "that sonofabitch" new manager Rob, and how he better stop breathing down his neck. Bill and I decide to fly back down to keep tabs on things. This way we can check out Casa Nueva's foundation too. The last time we were down, Bill had walked the hillside, the old horse pasture where the house would be.

"The placement of the house on the hill and the slope are critical to everything else," Bill explains. "Not just the view from it, but how it sits in and with the site."

When we get to La Finca, we drop our bags by the rubber tree and immediately go check out the new construction. Bill doesn't show surprise, disappointment, or most emotions like I do. I'm the type to blurt out a revealing sigh, or groan, or squeal. But with Bill, one often has to guess. Especially back then, I had to try to read those deep blue eyes of his.

The house, all two feet of its new foundation, looks good to me. But what do I know? There is a certain somberness in Bill's face, but maybe it's just the long flight.

"Everything cool?" I ask him later, as we unpack in our cabin.

"The whole thing is about three feet from where it's supposed to be, about three feet too close to the driveway. And it looks like they read the drawings wrong for the small cabin. It's a foot shorter in both directions. I'm not quite sure what's going on."

"Have you seen Rob's addition to the manager's cabin?"

"Yep, it's really ugly. And makes no sense."

"That's what I thought, like a big kite waiting for a hurricane."

Early the next morning, as that big old Vieques sun is rising, we wake to the sounds of nails and hammers, and noisy saws firing up.

"Good," I say. "I'm glad they get to work early. Guess they like to beat the heat." I am encouraged; that part of things seems to be going well.

"That's not our crew—that's the neighbors," Bill says, shrugging, as he makes the coffee.

I look out across the property to see the job site, still and quiet. "You're right, as usual. No sign of life up there. Some other lucky neighbor is getting their house built. Not us."

Neither of us has a clue why our crew doesn't arrive for another hour, maybe longer. The same thing happens the next day, and every day we are there.

Meanwhile Rob seems angry all the time. Everything about the island seems to be getting under his skin: the slow lines in the post office, the lack of choices in the grocery store, the broken gas pumps at the station, and, above all, Tito and his crew. Although theoretically he's not involved with the new house project, his distrust of the crew seems to be overwhelming him. He's supposed to be focusing on adding a second story to the manager's cabin.

"Just in case we get lucky, we'll have room for a baby," he says, and grins at me. I hope my inner shudder doesn't show.

Something doesn't feel right. Should I deal with all my questions around how a baby will work into their jobs and lives here? Or do I try to explain about the post office, the gas stations, and all that? Or do I deal with Tito? Will it bruise his male pride if we ask him why our crew starts later and now seems to quit earlier than any other? Is it our paranoia, or are they moving slowly throughout the day?

I don't want angry Rob to be right. And if I do talk to Tito, I might jinx things and make this whole miasma of bad juju even worse. Bad mojo, bad timing, bad work habits, bad management, bad communication. It seems sort of bad in every direction, so I put it out of my head. Anyway, it's hard to find Tito. He's rarely at the job site.

"Isn't he in charge of the crew?" I ask Bill, hoping he can explain.

"I thought so."

It's not the take-charge attitude I was looking for. I see that we are both feeling somewhat lost. Sitting down to do some work on the computer, I happen to come across a blog Rob is apparently drafting about life on Vieques. It smacks of cultural ignorance and racism. I am horrified. All I can think is, We have to fire him; we can't employ people who think like this. I call Anne for advice. She wonders if I misunderstood. Hopefully she's right. After all, Rob and his wife are competent in other areas.

And hopefully Tito is right too, when he reassures us later, over an evening's bottle of Spanish red, not to worry about nada—not even the sloping foundation Bill noticed. The concrete seems to follow the curve of the hill's slope rather than being leveled. Even I understand the concept of building on a good foundation, and the importance of being on the level. This doesn't look or feel good.

"*Todo está bien!* That's just the way we do it here. Don't you worry, I am like El Padrino. I'm the Godfather of the crew. They all know me. Everyone on the island knows me. I'm like the Godfather to the whole island."

Neither of us can figure out why Tito's popularity is relevant to the structure or how this should make us feel better. Apparently it has something to do with the clout he has, with the friend in the municipality and the paperwork that may or may not be needed someday.

After a week of paradise under our belts, Bill and I fly back to Seattle and our day jobs. We try to convince ourselves that everyone else is right—we so want them to be right. We want to be wrong about the ominous combination of fish and smoke we smell. We should be more trusting—of everybody, although none of them trust each other. Besides, there's no way we can keep flying back and forth like this. It will work out, we tell ourselves.

Only it doesn't. Weeks turn into months of delay, tens of thousands of dollars turn into much more. We are not only two times over budget building the house, we are months and more beyond schedule, with all the noise and chaos of construction now in the middle of high season.

Casa Nueva was supposed to be rented out to start paying for itself. But then it was also supposed to be a simple house to build. Tito is vague and miffed about everything we ask him. Rob continues to rant and froth about Tito and the whole island. The place is completely booked, as it always is in April.

Just a couple of weeks later I'm visiting my mom in Sonoma for the weekend when I wake one morning and notice a phone message that has come in overnight. Still half asleep, I press the little button: "Corky. Rob here. We're on the boat." Oh, good—my mind rushes to put things into context. They must have finally figured out how to take the ferry to do errands on the main island. I wonder who they got to look after the place for the day? We don't usually leave the island in high season.

Then I hear: "We are leaving. But don't worry; we left the place in good hands. One of our guests is up for managing the place. She's a software developer from Maine, so she's really responsible." That's when I fully wake up. "The situation had gotten out of hand. I feared for my wife's well-being. You know how to contact us if you need to. Goodbye."

I don't know how many times I play that message trying to make sense of it. I never have been able to. The next few hours, then days, then weeks are spent finding new managers—again. No, let's call them caretakers now. *Just take care of my baby. Please don't walk off the job in high season.*

First, however, the software developer, Jenny, calls and explains some of the mystery of the quick exit and the all-out war between the building crew and Rob. They thought he was a condescending bigot. There was open hostility between them. And poor Polly had miscarried. I am spared the details but can somehow feel the ugliness, sadness, and drama all the way to Seattle, over the phone lines. I feel responsible. I knew I should have fired that guy.

The fishy smell turned out to be fish. The smoke meant fire, too—and it burns. Tito had been a true friend, my best friend. Slowly, in bits and pieces, from friends and neighbors—even our accountant on the island—we hear that his crew and our project are sort of a joke. Everybody seems to know it, and now we know it too. We finally fire him.

We put the lead carpenter, José, in charge. He is easy to talk to. A month later he is arrested for not paying child support. Casa Nueva, Bill's beautiful design and our future winter retirement home, is finally built—but with such shoddy, careless work that it continues to break our hearts. It's also so far over budget we'll have to rent it out for years.

Tito stops by a month later while Anne is down from New York to see the house she's been funding . . . and funding. None of us feels comfortable enough to look him in the eye. Pouring a glass of wine doesn't feel right anymore. This man has ripped us off, misled us, and mismanaged our money, and the result is obvious—the bent beams and cracked foundation, light switches too high to reach, and uneven stair treads. The three of us stand on the deck with no idea how to behave with someone we once trusted as a friend. But Tito seems comfortable. He walks in, asks if we should share a little glass perhaps, and proceeds to tell us it is customary here to give a tip to the contractor at the end of the job.

As weird as it sounds, as ripped off as we were, I miss Tito. I miss our friendship. I miss his larger-than-life character, his evening glass of wine. It was so fun and handy to have Zorba and the Godfather sharing our jungle driveway, and all the more to have them rolled up in one. They don't make them like him anymore. We tried for a few years to get beyond it—forgive and forget and all that. But it was never the same. Eventually we all gave up. Last we heard, he was living in San Juan. His beautiful little home and outdoor kitchen are all overgrown now.

and lots of moving parts

and crannies

this place has lots of nooks

la finca caribe

la finca!

trying
to keep
things
together

16.

Another Day in Paradise

Polly and Rob's stint as managers was one of the worst and their exit in the middle of high season one of the hardest, with paying guests in every room and every cabin. New guests were checking in every day, and Jenny, a guest herself, was left in charge. Sadly, our bizarre caretaking legacy didn't stop here. The craziest part is that with each new hire I was my optimistic, Pollyanna self: These new guys will be the ones!

The next managers, from South Africa, sure seem like it: Jack and Tanya are awesome. They immigrated to Canada a few years ago and miss the warmer climate of their homeland. They are as friendly as they are handy. It appears that I've finally hired capable folks, and I can come to La Finca without having to work the whole time.

Jack and Tanya have been at the helm for a few months when I head down with Carrie, a girlfriend from Seattle. I am going to try and use the place like our guests do, for a vacation. What a concept! The relief I feel when I see the place is enormous. To find the finca safe and sound and—even better—as I left her, with no new wall murals or pets, no friends "living here, helping out for a while," no new major damage to the truck, is awesome. It's like coming home to your kids and the new babysitter. You're happy to see everything still standing.

To vacation at La Finca is a wondrous thing. I see why our guests like it. It feels indulgent to simply relax. Carrie and I spend our days swimming and snorkeling, reading and writing. Once the frogs kick in and the sun is low, we leave our hammocks to cook. Since it's low season, we take advantage of the privacy and share a few meals with Jack and Tanya on the big deck. The meals morph into evening card games and then into good talks about life, struggles, Buddhism. It feels great to enjoy the place as it's meant to be, with that wonderful mix of laughter and deep discussions. Perfect.

A few days into our stay Carrie and I are heading to the truck on our way to the beach when we bump into Jack and Tanya coming in from the gate. I'm carrying *After the Ecstasy, the Laundry* for my beach reading. It was that sort of time in my life.

"Oh, Jack," I say, "here's that book we talked about last night, if you want to borrow it."

Suddenly, out of nowhere, Jack, all six feet four inches and 250-plus pounds of him, turns to me, on me, in a full rage.

"That's what I can't stand about you! You and all other Americans! You're all hypocrites!" He is shouting, waving his arms and thrusting his face into mine. This is one of the most frightening moments of my life: His attack came out of nowhere, and I have no idea how bad it might get .

"You leave the rope lights on at night! How dare you call yourself an environmentalist? It's all bullshit!"

Jack's words make no sense. Where is this pent-up anger from? How did we get from my offering him a favorite Buddhist book to our nightlights? All I know is his wild rant is terrifying. Carrie is standing next to me, thank God, in the sunny patch next to the rubber tree, where everything had been so lovely thirty seconds before. She catches me when I almost swoon, her arms bracing me.

"Come on," she says, "we're getting out of here. Now."

Jack is still going on about my behavior. I don't know if we ran, or flew, to the truck. Carrie drives. I'm shaking. We are both in shock. We head to Sun Bay and the comfort of warm sand. We plow our legs into it. We spread our bodies across the salty white powder, hoping its heat can melt our tension. We jump into the water to wash away the bad vibes and fear. But nothing is really working.

"Could Jack get violent?" Carrie asks. "What's he going to do next?" She tries to help me figure out the next steps. "But Jesus, he's there and we're here! He has control of the place."

"And it's not like at home," I say. "It's not like I can call the police. It's not like the crazy gringa innkeeper fighting with her crazy gringo manager is going to be the top priority."

"What the hell do we do?"

Daylight is dwindling. We can't stay on the beach, and we have nothing with us. For practical as well as emotional reasons, being back at La Finca feels like the right first step. We decide to connect with Tanya, woman to woman.

"Oh, don't worry too much about Jack. He just gets a bit testy sometimes. Of course it's safe for you here!" she says with a laugh, brushing it all off as we tiptoe back onto the property.

Apparently we are weirdos who overreacted. Hoping she's right, I scurry back into the casita. Like the beach, La Finca is healing. Being home helps. The swoosh of the

i have known this place
as rows of
dominoes fall. years
dreams crumble.
toasters rust
guests leave.
friends come. ~~friends~~
~~cancer~~ in every bone annie (has is annual
~~good books~~ leave. new ones arrive.

down

ve.

always the
and

new dreams ~~f~~

branches against the roof combs away my fears. Tiene Leche, our cat who usually keeps her distance, stops by to make sure we're okay.

Jack and Tanya join us too, awkwardly. "You see," Jack says, trying to get comfortable on one of our small rickety chairs on the casita deck. "My family lived way out in a small rural township. My best friends were all Zulus. South Africa was under apartheid. I witnessed it all."

"Jack suffers from serious posttraumatic stress," Tanya explains. "So he can get a little angry when he feels pressured. No hard feelings, okay?"

It seems that Jack's bad mood had been triggered by a Pictionary game we played together the night before, where he hadn't done so well and I had. I'm not one to remember those things. He apparently is. It all makes sense, sort of—in an abstract, distant, beyond-my-wildest-imagination sort of way.

Carrie and I talk about nothing else as we fly back to Seattle. Nice folks, smart, creative. But I can't stop worrying about what guest might set Jack off next. Thank God it's the slow season—no one will be there for a while yet. Vieques was like that back then. For all of September and most of October, much of the island shut down. Good time to get projects done. This year it would give me time to come up with a solution.

Tanya calls a few weeks later, saying something convoluted about someone on the island not liking them and turning them in for having improper work visas from Canada. I've never heard of anyone being turned in for anything in Puerto Rico. She claims that they've had to leave very quickly.

I am not sad to see them go. I've been having my own posttraumatic stress whenever I talk with them. Even over the phone, from Seattle, I'm cautious not to say anything that sounds the least bit competitive, Buddhist, environmental, American, or hypocritical.

They are gone, and once again I am on the quick lookout for new caretakers.

Oh, Lordy, I'm tired of this. It feels like I've seen it all. There are caretakers who don't bother to tell me when they break up or friends move in for a month or two, when they're pregnant, or when the travel columnist from the *New York Times* stays with us for three days. "Oh, sorry, I didn't know you'd care." Did they arrive normal and get worn down by the island? Or was it the finca? We'd had great caretakers too, of course, but they didn't seem to last. They had other lives to lead, boats to sail away on, other adventures beckoning. It's not like I couldn't relate to that.

My notorious optimism is wearing thin when, lo and behold, *Gracias á Dios!* Somehow, through fate and Craigslist, we find Marisol and Juan Carlos. They both grew up in the hills of central Puerto Rico and went to college in the States. They're clearly young and earnest.

"We love your place!" Marisol gushes in perfect English, with a beautiful, provincial Puerto Rican accent. "We want to learn everything we can from you. Eventually we want to open our own eco-inn on the main island."

Bill and I like the sound of being respected. It feels good. Juan Carlos and Marisol eagerly shadow us for a week, and then there's the week of training, before we shadow them for a last week. They are eager to learn and do it all.

Changing planes in Atlanta, on our way back to Seattle, I notice that emails I'd sent from San Juan haven't been replied to. "Give them a break, Corks," Bill says, trying to reassure me.

"Hey, I'm basically optimistic, but by this time at least I know when it's weird. These emails are important. They're about large groups who need info."

"Give them a little time," Bill says.

I love his kindness, but I'm not convinced. Communication stays sluggish. Maybe it's a cultural thing. Maybe they don't have my neurotic sense of urgency. As I am learning how to cope with this new tempo, the trickle stops trickling. It's been two weeks since we left. In a few days, an important group I've been courting, wrangling, and wanting to get to La Finca for over a year will be arriving. They are executive directors of influential NGOs in Boston, all potentially important to La Finca for business and to Vieques for community development and organizing. I am so bummed that I can't be there for the group, as I feel like I've gotten to know them. I want everything to be right. Juana Carlos and Marisol are probably tired of my checking the details, but this is also the first time we will be working with Sylvia and her foodie friend from San Juan to do the catering. There are lots of details to button down, and now nothing. Not slow, just no response.

"GUYS...HATE TO BUG YOU AGAIN. BUT WONDERING IF PHONE OR INTERNET IS OUT. PLEASE PING ME BACK IF/ WHEN YOU GET THIS. THX :-) c"

Nada back for another day. What's the part about not being able to run a business from four thousand miles away?

Even Bill agrees it is getting weird. It's coming up on two full days of no contact. On top of this, I'm due to fly to Sonoma for my sister Valerie's sixtieth birthday. Bill stays home for what will be a quick weekend away, such a fast turnaround that I barely pack a thing, not even a book and not much more than a change of clothes. But sadly, at what should be a fun get-together with old friends from home, I'm spending a good chunk of the time on the phone, trying to connect to our caretakers.

Swallowing my pride and fear, I call our friend and neighbor Helena. I try to sound confident, professional. "I'm sure they're all right," I say. "But I'd love it if you could just go check on them. I know there aren't any guests right now. But we've got this important group coming Monday."

An hour later Helena calls me back. "Corks," she says, "I'm not sure what to tell you. It's hard to figure. They are definitely not there. Your truck is gone, but the car is there. What's weirder, it's like they should be there. I mean the doors are open, the lights are on in the middle of the day, and fans are on in empty rooms. And on the laundry porch, there is the largest pile of dirty laundry I've ever seen. Just sitting there. It's like it all stopped in action—creepy."

"Thanks," I manage to gulp. I try to swallow. It's harder to pull off the confident professional vibe I've been trying to assume. "Thanks a bunch."

"Okay, Big Sis, which horror do I deal with first?" I say to Val. "The very real potential of a kidnapping? Some other violent crime? What do I do?"

But Val is trying to have a good time with her pals. My finca is my problem. Over the years my ongoing finca crises have morphed from family entertainment to ennui. I'm in the corner either on the phone or in a daze. Or both.

In the States you could imagine Juan Carlos and Marisol taking off. On Vieques, though, there's nowhere to go. And they couldn't get a ferry reservation that quickly. Besides, why take the junky truck and not the car? One thing I do know is that dirty wet laundry is not to be left in large piles in hot weather. In my mind's eye I'm seeing the mold grow. I'll call Sal and see if she can get up there and at least start cleaning.

Thank God for Sal, a good friend who's my age and one of those rare finds on the island: steady, reliable, and resourceful. Honest, no drama. She has become an all-around Girl Friday for us as she gets her own property management company going. Plus, she's reasonable. She charges a flat fifteen dollars to clean or run errands. A short while after I call, Sal is en route to La Finca. And after the party in Sonoma, my sister drives me to the airport. It's not like we can wait until Monday to get things sorted out—this is really too big and too frightening to process.

"What about the office? The safe? The computer? Were we robbed? And the property? Oh, my God—the pool. Yikes, how long since it's been cleaned?"

Val can't answer my questions, but she gives me some clean clothes and a book to read on the plane.

As she drives away I am visualizing the algae bloom thickening the pool water, and I can't tell if I'm feeling very much the grown-up superwoman or the frightened little girl. At the airport I rush to buy my first-ever last-minute, one-way flight, without any luggage. It's weird—it makes my role clearer: I'm James Bond, or the *Mission Impossible* guy, who dashes up to the ticket counter just before boarding. Never a suitcase to be seen, and yet they always have whatever they need.

As I'm running to my flight, my cell phone rings. "Corky! It's Janine and Ricky!"—other newish island friends. "Oh my God, girlfriend. We just heard from Helena about what's going on up at your place! You should have called." Gotta love how fast news travels on a small island despite its sketchy cell service. "We are here to help! We can go up there right now. Can't we, Ricky?" Janine has been pushing to establish our new friendship for a while.

"Thanks, Jan. I've hired Sal—she's there now to get things ready for this group coming. I'm paying her fifteen dollars an hour, if that works for you too. Plus, I have to find my managers."

"You bet, pal. Don't even talk business stuff. We are here for you, buddy! We'll spend the night up there. Just to keep the place safe."

In the film world, this is called foreshadowing, a little tip-off of the doom that lies ahead. You may not have noticed the lock that was stuck for a second, the car that wouldn't start, the wind that kicked up. I'm not paying attention—I'm getting on the plane.

"Oh, that's okay." But I'm not sure she hears me.

I call from Newark in between flights and learn that Juan Carlos and Marisol have been found, safe and sound. They are in our parking lot casually taking two kayaks off the jeep. They are more than surprised to see the place taken over by a small team scurrying around making beds, cleaning fridges, doing laundry. They explain it all: They had gone kayaking for a few days. Hadn't told anyone, hadn't secured the property.

"I think you are really overreacting," Marisol says to me, on the phone from Newark. "We were going to get the place ready this evening."

I summon my nerves of steel and fire them over the phone. Two weeks on the job, and no plan in sight for me.

"You can't fire us! We quit!"

Okay. Guess that worked out.

Next Ricky wants to talk to me. "Hey, Corky," he says. "This scene is really intense up here. Super-bad vibes with these two. And the mess, you wouldn't believe it."

He's been saying that for over a day now. How bad can it still be?

"Janine is really stressing out. She's doing everything she can, and I am too. But the mental anguish of sleeping here. We didn't sleep a wink last night, and now we're back at it. The mess, you can't believe the mess. So we're going to charge you. We've been talking about it. It's only fair."

"Of course it's fair, Ricky," I say. "I told you guys to, and I appreciate you jumping in. Be sure to charge me for both of your hours for whatever time it takes, yesterday and today. Just double the fifteen dollars I'm paying Sal, for the two of you." Seems straightforward enough.

"Yeah, that's what we've been talking about. You pay Sal fifteen dollars because that's her hourly. Janine is a licensed massage therapist. She makes forty-five an hour. It's only fair that she, that we, be compensated for the sleepless night and the hours we were here tossing and turning. We wouldn't just leave the place, or you, stranded."

Things are starting to swirl. Once again I'm Alice freefalling past Mad Hatters and clocks while the Cheshire cat grins. "What are you saying?"

"Wow, Corky. Don't get all defensive. I'm just trying to be straight with you. We've been leading the charge here. So far we are at $2,800, when you add it up."

"What?" Alice thumps hard, onto what she hopes is rock bottom.

"It's simple. That's Jan's hourly times two—for the each of us, that's ninety dollars for every hour we've been here. It is only fair we're paid for being on guard all night. And the mess, you wouldn't believe the mess. Dude, I can't even tell you how bad and, really, how stressful it is."

"Ricky, listen to me. It's Sunday, ten a.m. I want you both off the property. I'm not paying you ninety dollars an hour to sleep or not sleep there, and I'm not paying you for any time after ten a.m. Sunday. Please leave now."

By the time I get to the island, in Ricky and Janine's minds they have somehow racked up yet another $800 and left a bill for $3,500. I don't have a clue what's going on with them. All I know is I'm there just soon enough to look around and thank Helena and Sylvia for saving the day before I walk out to the gate to welcome the dignitaries in. They spend five happy days there, for their annual retreat and summit, never the wiser.

Such is the life of the innkeeper. At least this one. At least at this inn.

17.

No Stopping This Carnival

Back in Seattle, things seem to be rolling out smoothly. Bill and I move into a new house we bought together. Our kids on both sides are healthy and happy, settling into their lives. I am working and getting back on my feet financially despite the crazy bills that accrued at La Finca. I'm happy to have turned things around, but I cannot, for the life of me, get La Finca's hiring thing right. Hiring and managing people is a big part of my day-to-day work life in Seattle. Why can't I get it right at La Finca?

It's gray and rainy in Seattle, another wet weekend. All Bill and I have to do is solve this La Finca problem. "It's insane! Or we are," I say. "I really don't know how much longer I can do this. Or how many more versions of it I can handle."

Looking south from here, everything seems pretty bleak. I'm used to seeing my way out, even if it's vaguely lit or off in the distance. Right now I don't have a clue.

"What's that quote about insanity meaning doing the same thing over and over again but wanting different results?" Bill is trying to be helpful as he reads the paper over coffee.

I continue to search the leaden skies for a way out. "You're right," I say. "We cannot do it anymore. We just can't. But what the heck do we do instead?"

We bounce around all sorts of ideas and business models. "We could close the place down to the public and rent it as self-serve vacation property to friends and past guests," I say.

"Or maybe make the manager's role more caretaking the place, less of a job job and more like rotating friends who manage it for a few months. All our friends are starting to retire. Who wouldn't want to spend a couple of months at La Finca?" Bill says.

"You're right." I like where he's going with this. "If it was run by buds, even a collection of them, coming in and out, it would be easier. We need to know the folks there so we can know what's going on." This sounds like a good plan.

Since this is before social media became the primary form of networking, I tell everyone I know, hoping to build a network of interested, good folks. Two weeks later we have results.

After work one evening, I share the good news with Bill. "Jamie is a friend of Lisa's. She's awesome. This plan of hiring friends of friends may be working."

Bill is as relieved as I am. "I know," he says. "She and Brian could be the ticket. She can do everything, from cooking and housekeeping to online marketing, and has all the energy in the world. Plus Brian specializes in alternative energy and green construction. What if we actually got our solar projects going?" I allow myself to fantasize that this might last.

"And they both speak Spanish, for God's sake," I add.

Jamie is a remarkable woman. We have mutual friends and clients who all share the same sense of awe at her talents. She is exceptionally bright and positive but equally resourceful, strategic, and self-reliant. Her one-woman company, Your Girl Friday, is a personal assistant business. She is hired by all kinds of people in the Seattle area to do all kinds of things, from tax preparation and detailed office organization to estate sale planning, catering small special events, and even dog walking. Plus she runs it all on this funny thing called a Blackberry. No one else I know even has one. She's matter-of-fact, ahead of the curve, and still fun, one of those rare know-it-alls you can't help but love because they are cheerful and just happen to *actually* know it all. Oh, and she's an avid recycler, committed to a simple, healthy living. She gets it.

Jamie and Brian ask us to dinner. They live in Fremont, Seattle's arty offbeat neighborhood just south of us. Bill and I will discuss the job with them again, now that we've sent the thirteen-page job description along with its daily, weekly, and monthly duties. If that hasn't scared them away, nothing will. The neighborhood, the apartment's upcycled creative charm, the food—it all feels so good. More than an omen, it just feels right. Over a fabulous meal—the kind Jamie is known for—Brian in his humble, southern way explains that even though he just got promoted, and even though Jamie's business is booming, they want this last chance at an opportunity for real adventure before they really settle down.

"What about the hardship factor?" I say. It's a little tough for me to imagine this bubbly gal handling the ongoing intensity of tropical life. "The relentlessness of the weather and the demands? It never ends. It can wear you out, even if from the outside it all looks like paradise."

"Good question, and no problem." Jamie pauses and gives Brian a knowing smile. "There's something you don't know about me."

Their cozy and lively apartment seems to quiet down. Brian gets up to start clearing the table.

"I was born a ward of the courts," Jamie says. "My birth mother was incarcerated. By the time I was eighteen I had lived in twelve different foster homes. On my eighteenth birthday I was given twenty dollars and my freedom to leave. I walked out of Albuquerque and made a promise to myself that I'd never look, or go, back. I'd just walk out of town and be the happiest person I could possibly be. I know all about overcoming adversity. Not a problem."

My mind goes blank. My heart breaks. Bill and I look at each other and give Jamie the kind of loving smile you give a friend when they've lost someone, because it's all you can do.

She could certainly handle whatever hassles La Finca and life on Vieques might throw at her. Leaky roofs and no gas at the station seem like small potatoes next to what she's described.

Jamie and Brian's first year at La Finca was like most things they take on—remarkable. Between her office skills and marketing savvy and Brian's can-do attitude and construction know-how, they get more things done than we could have dreamed of. I'm regularly on the phone with her, or swapping emails, about various projects; Bill works with Brian. Anne, in New York, loves hearing about the progress. Jamie and Brian have friends from the States come down for solar project installations. Guests love them. They, and La Finca, are getting the love, care, and smarts they deserve and need.

Sharing the finca is all I ever wanted out of this magic place—sharing it with guests, guests who come back again and again, guests who become friends, friends from Puerto Rico, from the States, from Europe, the folks who run it, the neighbors, the Viequense kids we give summer camp stays to, the college kids we give trade-out stays to. Letting the place build its own community. The feeling of relief from the hard work and years it took to get here is enormous. Joy. As it should be. The place is so much fun to run when it's all working.

And then they break up. "Brian is going back to the States. Like, to stay," Jamie tells me on the phone.

I'm sure I heard it wrong. A knot forms at the top of my gut. "It's over" is all that comes to mind. The how and why—both so unbelievable—are not my business, but La Finca is.

Jamie knows what I'm thinking. "I know it's always been a two-person job, Corky," she says. "But I really want to stay, and I have a plan, a way for me to do it on my own."

Nothing from me yet, so she goes on. "We take Brian's salary and use that to hire out for repairs and maintenance work. And honestly I've made so many friends here, people will trade out fixing something for a good meal. So sometimes it won't cost you a thing."

Jamie is showing her remarkably resourceful sense, but she's also sounding unnaturally businesslike. That's okay. I recognize the coping skill. It'll be fine.

And it is. We aren't there to watch, but Jamie takes both reins in her capable hands. We are in touch and in sync. In addition to the guests, she wins the hearts and minds of our island and Puerto Rico friends. Like Sylvia in San Juan, Victoria, our best friend from Ponce, started as a guest, very early on. Both Victoria and Sylvia claim to have met every manager/caretaker we've ever had. They know the place inside and out and love it dearly. Victoria in particular gets very close to Jamie.

"This time, chica, this time you have a winner," she tells me. "We loved Brian too. But Jamie is amazing. When she gets a vacation, I've promised to take her to Spain with us. You don't mind sharing her, do you, amiga? My girls adore her."

Truth is, I don't mind sharing at all. It's fine with me. When things are running this well, a happy manager means a happy finca and happy guests. Taking advantage of the extra time in the slow season, Jamie starts doing more catering, "I pulled off a fresh lobster dinner for thirty. I'm becoming known as the best caterer on Vieques," she says.

Anne, the longtime restaurateur, is almost incredulous when I update her during one of our weekly calls.

"Yeah," I say, "I thought it sounded a little over the top myself. Not to mention there are some really good caterers on the island."

"Hey, give her a break," Bill says, overhearing me. "Have you ever seen anything Jamie couldn't do? And exceedingly well?"

A ROGUES' GALLERY OF OUR MOST ILLUSTRIOUS STAFF & residents, guests, and others who just stop in...

"Bill's right," I tell Anne. "She is somewhat superhuman. If any one person can do it all, Jamie can. Heck, she's singlehandedly running the place."

If I were a mystery writer, things might be different. I'd have the mystery structure down: the build-up, the mystery, and then the resolution. But with La Finca, it's different: The stories, the oh-so-many stories, are just there. They just happen, and more often than not, as you may have noticed, there is no big reveal, no answer or explanation. Sometimes there's not even a flipping clue about what really happened, let alone why. Apparently I've forgotten my note to self regarding *porque* and *por qué*. Better read it again.

The first hint of anything odd is the disappearance of the tea towels, of all things. Artwork doesn't last in our climate. Bugs, mold, rust—things eat away the print, the painting, even the frame. Insects work their way between the glass and the artwork; I'll never know how or why. Unframed art is just as bad. Thumbtacks rust in the corners, the paper deteriorates in the heat and moisture. Things curl and fall off the wall, or they don't and you wish they would.

So I get smart. I discover that linen dishcloths actually last. To add a bit of color and texture to our barebones walls and simple rooms, I pin up a few funky ones from the 1960s, some with images of Vera Graphic fruit my mom had given to me, and voilà!— Finca Caribe style. Over the years I collect enough vintage tropical island–themed tea

towels for each room to have its own: Cuba, the Bahamas, tropical fruit, hula girls, all from the 1940s to the 1970s. Nothing of importance to anyone but me, as I know the value of anything that lasts.

On one trip down I notice that Room 6 is missing its Tahiti cloth. Maybe it got moved to another room. Weirder things have happened. That's when I discover that all of the rooms are missing their tea towels.

"Oh, a friend of mine was here a while back," Jamie says, when I ask her about them. "She's worked in a lot of inns, and she didn't think they went with our look. She's really good at knowing what looks good, and what our guests want."

Whether it's a friend, a coworker, or an employee, when someone you know says something that makes no sense, it's an odd feeling. Responding with logic to an illogical comment seems useless at best. Sadness swirls with frustration into confusion. I feel insulted and even violated. It's hard to know what course of action to take.

"That's weird." I get that much out. "Do you know where they are? I'd like to put them back up."

"Hmm," Jamie says. "I actually haven't seen them. But I'm sure they're around here somewhere."

That seems out of character for her. Sweet, helpful Jamie doesn't seem to care.

Duuuun *dun*. Duuuun *dun*. The Jaws theme song starts up in my head.

"Hey, Jamie, before you leave, where's the bright orange bookshelf?" I say. "The one from Casa Nueva. I'm thinking it would work well in the new casita."

Our furniture has a long tradition of moving from room to room, and from house to house, between my visits. Groups do amazingly interesting things and sometimes feel the need to hijack one thing for another, so the missing shelf doesn't faze me for a second.

"What orange bookshelf?" Jamie says. "I don't remember ever seeing an orange one. We have a purple one. Are you getting confused?"

The soundtrack in my head gets louder.

The next day I'm looking for a brochure for a couple who stops by to check out the place. There are none to be found, anywhere. Even the reserve pile is gone.

Jamie shrugs it off. "We just ran out. When Tyler and his friends were down, they kept using them as scratch paper for keeping score during games. Guess we better order some new ones."

When Ty calls to check in, I cut to the chase. "Hey, hon, did you guys play a lot of cards when you were here? I mean, you know better than to use up the printed brochures for your scorecards, right?"

"Huh? Mom, we didn't play cards—or any other games. I don't know what you're talking about. But does it have anything to do with your friend who is caretaking the place? She's weird. She out-parties me and my gang. Jesus, she didn't come home until the middle of the night, for several nights in a row. Sometimes not until the next morning. The weirdest part was the look in her eyes."

Why would Jamie fabricate this story about Ty using up the brochures? Why hadn't she ordered more, or even noticed we were out? She's always seemed to be in control of everything.

I can't ask her now. She's in New York for a break. She's supposed to see Anne, but there's confusion about meeting times and dates.

"I was looking forward to seeing her last night at the restaurant," Anne says, "but apparently I had the wrong day. She never showed."

"I thought you guys were seeing each other a couple of days ago." I say. I'm still trying to sort out what's going on. I don't want to burden Anne with missing tea towels or false accusations about brochures.

"Yeah, she changed our lunch plans a couple of times," Anne says. "Sort of odd. I guess she's really busy."

I'm wondering how long we can all continue to give Jamie the benefit of growing doubts. In the meantime we're holding the fort.

One afternoon I'm at the manager's desk taking a reservation. It's hot and breezy, as usual, and Tiene Leche is asleep in the in-basket. The desk is its own slightly messy hodgepodge of calendars and files, business cards, and receipts. It works, though.

Usually Jamie has it super-tidy. I think she may be a little OCD. She has redone the cleaning checklist for every house and room, and the level of detail floors me. I've asked her about the necessity of spelling out every step, but she's adamant. Oh, well, go for it. Checklist your heart out.

But what's this? I see a small plastic folder I don't recognize stuck behind some papers in one of the milk crates we use as a file cabinet. It's labeled "How to Housesit La Finca Caribe."

We already have the Bible, a big red plastic three-ring binder with information on everything from pool cleaning and pump flow charts to neighbors' phone numbers, hurricane preparation, the guy in Berkeley who sells us our mosquito nets wholesale. Every detail we need to reference about running the place is in this binder. Keyword: we.

So who is this for? Who housesits La Finca? When the manager is gone, we're here. Or are we?

I finally get it. Jamie has been farming out her job for who knows how long to heaven only knows who! Her housesitting guide is the most carefully detailed checklist on how to run La Finca. *My* business. Jamie wasn't even giving them the Bible, which would have ensured that things were done the way we wanted them done. Nope. She had rewritten

THE GUEST HOUSE

This being human is a guest house.
Every morning a new arrival.

A joy, a depression, a meanness,
some momentary awareness comes
as an unexpected visitor.

Welcome and entertain them all!
Even if they are a crowd of sorrows,
who violently sweep your house
empty of its furniture,
still, treat each guest honorably.
He may be clearing you out
for some new delight.

The dark thought, the shame,
the malice,
meet them at the door
laughing and invite them in.

Be grateful for whatever comes,
because each has been sent
as a guide from beyond.

— Jellaludin Rumi,
translation by Coleman Barks

Rumi's parents had to be inkeepers...

every step so that her submanagers would do them the way she wanted them done.

Bill and I are still scratching our heads a few hours later over drinks in town. Sure enough, the barmaid hears us mention La Finca Caribe and says, "Oh, I love that place! I've managed it."

A day or two later Bill meets another woman out paddleboarding.

"Really? You're the owner?" she says. "I had no idea, I thought Jamie owned it. I've stayed there a couple of times, you know, when she was away."

We learn to stay calm and friendly yet clear when we tell people we are the owners. Each time I find myself wondering, Are you the gal who took down my tea towels? Did you sell them on eBay? Or the handmade wire sculpture of Don Quixote, or my enormous fossilized emperor's shell, or that darn orange bookshelf?

Jamie's cunning went even further. Her request to get rid of the archaic landline and have incoming calls forwarded to her cell phone was brilliant. She had explained to us that she would be able to answer calls even if she was in Isabel Segunda getting supplies. It turns out she was doing that, but from Philly or NYC or wherever she'd go to hear her favorite bands. She was really into Phish.

It's not like asking her is going to shed any more light on this. Ty was so right about the look in her eye. Weird, indeed. Our mutual friends in Seattle feel her slip away from them too. No one understands. Interestingly, Jamie gives notice just as all is unraveling. She's been offered a job running a newer, trendier hotel on the island.

Eventually they will have their own Jamie stories, as will the handful of Vieques friends she does property management for. There are tales of them coming home to missing furniture and appliances, and her legacy spreads around the island. Who knows how much is gossip? She ends up leaving the island, who knows why? Drugs? A shadow legacy of the walk out of Albuquerque, or was that all made up? The thirty lobster dinners, was any of it true?

You can wonder why forever and not make much progress. All we know for sure is that our plan of hiring friends isn't working. Soon we'll be able to be there, if not full time then enough to escape our winters and handle the bulk of high season. The plan is shimmering on the horizon, almost within grasp—but it could be a mirage. Xing Ji has another year of high school, and I've only been back at work for a few years, so financially I'm not ready to leave yet. Bill loves his work and shows little interest in bailing on his career just yet.

In the meantime, Bill's daughter Jess, her husband, Rory, and their toddler Avery are looking for one last working adventure before settling down. Rory and Jess are whitewater kayak guides. They work with the eco-adventure sort of public who make up our guests, and they speak Spanish. And they are available. After a round of questions and answers, they are on board.

Having family at La Finca is a wonderful feeling; the relief is amazing. Everything works like it should. Bill and I have a team to bounce project ideas and priorities off of. Partnership. The four of us plan, talk, and laugh—with respect, trust, and love to boot. The finca finally is operating like the family business it was always meant to be. Jess and Rory are as happy as we are. Guests are happy. Master Avery is very happy toddling about in his tropical home, entertaining and endearing the guests.

Like a sailboat, slowly, pointing up into the wind, settling down, slow and steady, creaking, moaning, things fall into place. You can almost hear them land where they belong. And then it's quiet. In a good way. The creaking and groaning is over. We're on course.

Six months later Jess and Rory find out they are expecting a second child and decide it's time to return to the States. We are almost within reach of being able to go ourselves, but to fill the gap Tyler and his girlfriend Terra step in. The handful of months between Tyler's commercial fishing work in Alaska and Terra's school schedule cover us just long enough. The plan happens: Remote management is over, at least for a while. Bill and I head down to run the place full time for a season.

We'll be at the helm of my sweet, patient finca for the winter, the Caribbean's high season, for four months. Although they comprise only a third of the year, the months between Christmas and Easter represent the lion's share of our business. After fifteen years of owning the place, I will be innkeeper. If things go south or turn sour, it's our doing. It's our circus, our rodeo. I've been preparing for this for a long, long time.

Smooth Sailing

I stare out at the forms and etched patterns of frozen white landscapes far below our plane. How many times have I made this flight from Seattle to San Juan? I've never been this excited before, never been so sure I was doing the right thing. Already winter seems to be distancing itself from me. Or me from it.

I work on being more present in the moment. When I fully channel La Finca, I come to a sweet realization. The place responds to the hands-on physical structural attention. La Finca is like Tiene Leche, arching her back for a longer pet. She shines and purrs in hope and anticipation of more.

"I guess this means we're snowbirds, or rainbirds," I say to no one. Bill is asleep, and besides, he wouldn't want to be called a snowbird any more than he wanted to be called retired. I'm okay with being a bird; I am flying south for the season. Winter, the holidays, even my kids, they will all forgive me for leaving. I'm doing what I need, and want, to be doing—somehow, like I always knew I would. My calling is calling. It has always been calling, but now I am able to fully answer.

Coming down three weeks before the Christmas clock strikes and the tidal wave of holiday travel commences gives us just enough time to get settled, make last-minute repairs, and maybe get in a quick construction project. Then, voilà, one week before Christmas Day, one day after schools let out, the curtain rises and the wonderful craziness begins. It's all so predictable now, but it wasn't back then. Now I know the pattern of the influx of guests—who is likely to come when and need what. Cozy family reunions come at Christmas, more party-loving groups of friends come for New Year's, and the Browns come every year for a stay in Casa Nueva the week in between.

Back then we were caught off guard by the severity of the change, from having the place quiet and to ourselves suddenly filled to capacity. It happens overnight and takes place all across the island. The hardware stores, restaurants, gas stations, and beaches are all busy. We were both nervous and excited; happy to be there and meet them all, happy to help anyone with any question. More often than not, for returning guests, it is finally clarified who actually owns the place.

"Oh, you're the owner! I've always heard there was one," or "I've heard about you!" Many guests, like the Browns, have been coming for years. I hate to call them typical, but they do represent our clientele. She works at a university, he's the stay-at-home dad, and Dexter, their adorable son, has been spending the holidays with us for half of his ten years on the planet. They've seen the place in its different eras. Bill and I sit on the deck, over coffee in the morning or a beer in the evening, and swap stories with them. Some memories cause me to shudder; sometimes I laugh.

First-time guests have very different, equally challenging questions: Why is the island out of gas? How long does the Three Kings' Day celebration last? When will we be able to rent a car? Is it safe to ride a scooter? We have a lot to learn, like being able to sound smart and helpful and patient, when we might not feel like any of these things. Are the ferries on time? My phone's weather app shows a cloud and rain icon for every day we're here. Should we be worried?

It's as though we are kids playing house, making a clubhouse, but instead it's playing hotel on a deserted island. "Just ask yourself, What would Swiss Family Robinson do? Or maybe Gilligan," I tell Bill. "That's perfect, honey. You're the professor, I'm Mary Ann." We're not quite Robinson Crusoe, but inventive scrappiness helps.

"Hey, is this milk crate I found under the house too funky to use as the front desk organizer?"

"Don't think so." Bill is turning a rusty cast-iron sink we found in the shrubs into a planter on the deck. "Nothing here is too funky. I think people come here for the funk." He's right, and thank God they do.

Bill heads up our maintenance and facilities department. It's a department of one: him. Oh, and there's the pool boy—that's Bill too. I head up sales and marketing, housekeeping, and catering, so to speak. It usually means me cooking a meal for sixteen that I'd usually just cook for the two of us. We both handle the concierge, guest services, and front desk functions for arrivals and check-out—whichever one of us is closest to the gate when the *público* pulls up.

We're having a ball making it up as we go, and when we can't, I get adept at making trades with guests. I've always offered free stays to friends for our preseason weeklong work parties. Now I learn to offer a beer to tech-savvy guests who can get our printer working or explain cloud computing to me as we watch the afternoon skies drift along from the deck.

I get pretty good at spotting inherent skill sets, as well as vacation preferences. Some folks don't want to work on vacation. Others love to be asked, to do something useful or be involved more closely with the finca. It's not uncommon, even without solicitation from me, for a guest, whether cabinetmaker or landscape designer, to offer to lend a hand with whatever project we are tackling—making a bottle wall, putting in new stepping stones, painting a couch. Before long I realize I can offer entire free stays to these kinds of worker bees. I start sending an email once or twice a year asking if anyone wants a free stay in exchange for working mornings, pruning the nightmare that's overtaking the family cabaña, or building a fence out of pallets. Folks offer up and become regular guests, then friends, often coming back every year or two. They are part of the family.

We get to know what works and what doesn't. There's so much to learn and unlearn that I lose track. The best is the reward for unlearning what you're supposed to do and seeing how well it works to do what you want to do. I hate paying the bank fee for credit card transactions, especially with margins as thin as ours. I don't mind paying taxes, in hopes they might go to all that's in need around us: schools, roads, hospitals. But card fees are a different story.

"We aren't going to take cards anymore—it's cash only, pay as you go," I declare. Even my family and friends think this is maybe too much to ask of guests. It must be winter 2011, because as soon as I explain this to guests as our own little Occupy effort, they don't seem to mind. If they do, of course we capitulate and take their card. We learn the direct benefit of going with the flow: One guest loves the morning sun, the next shuns it, and there's no way to know which it will be. In the long run we still save money.

Depending on the day's activities, I'm covered in a film of sweat, dust, or dirt when I fall back onto the manager's cabin deck couch in the evening, the lazy cats reluctantly scattering as I drop. This couch has been painted and repainted a handful of times. It's a tad too funky to keep inside, even for me. So it lives out on our deck, high above the banana grove, facing southwest. Even though I'm too exhausted to appreciate much, I take in the beauty of the evening sky. The frogs and crickets are starting to get serious about their evening soundtrack.

If playing crosswords and Sudoku keeps your brain strong, we have nothing to worry about. Bill seems to love it all, the learning and the working, as much as I do. We are reaping and enjoying the fruits of our labors—and working our asses off. Twelve-hour days are common. The boundary between work and play is so blurred that we stop trying to separate the two.

"Honey, I'm too tired to cook," I say.

"No problem." Bill is all over it. "We'll go out. The finca owes us something for over-time pay."

"But, honey, I'm too tired to walk to the truck."

Thank God for the hummus and fancy cheese Room 3 left for us. That and a couple of cold Medallas, the watery but oh-so-refreshing local beer, will get us through another evening.

Luckily this is all as fun as it is hard. I read in some silly bed-and-breakfast blog about the importance of having a crockpot with some soup or chili for late-night check-ins. Great idea. We switch it up a little to offer our version of Puerto Rican rice and beans. We enact our welcome dinner tradition so incoming guests can relax after the long day's travel. And if we're cooking, we might as well invite the folks already here. Everybody loves it. It breaks the ice. We don't have to be the only tour guides; the guests who've been exploring for three days love to share their island savvy with the arriving travelers. Folks with kids meet the other kids. People from Brooklyn compare where they shop and go to yoga class.

We learn that most people are reluctant to break down these barriers on their own, especially on their first night and sometimes for days, or all of their stay. But at the same time they are grateful to be gently ushered into it by our efforts. People want to connect. This knowledge comes in handy when we are looking at a looming catastrophe one Christmas week.

It's the first time I can remember that the main house isn't rented to one large group or family for the week. Christmas is probably the busiest week of the year for the island, so unusual things can happen. This year all six rooms book up with six different parties. One large family get-together doesn't usually mind or even notice sharing two bathrooms or our thin plywood walls. But Bill and I can see the potential tensions—and certainly the awkwardness—of six groups of strangers arriving the same preholiday weekend.

Then it dawns on me. Because we held out so long waiting for the large family group booking that never came, all six different parties in the main house booked late—just in the last few weeks, when we had given up on finding a group. During the holidays on Vieques, that means none of the six parties will have a rental car. Back then the island can easily book all the cars for Christmas visitors by late September. No matter how much late-booking guests try, they won't find an available car.

Usually we can help folks navigate around without cars, even from our location three miles outside Esperanza. We hook them up with our favorite público drivers who are dependable and reasonable or connect them with other guests with cars who can give them a lift. We explain that they can easily grab a *público* back up from town or the beach.

"Hey, Bill," I say, "what are we going to do about Christmas?"

"Oh, Corks, I thought we weren't giving gifts. I like that we graduated beyond that whole thing. No gifts? No worries, hon."

"Dude, I'm talking about the main house. All these folks without cars. No *público* is going to work over Christmas. It's going to be terrible for them. They are all going to be miserable. Oh yeah, and we can't go to Val and Franz's for Christmas dinner. We can't just leave everyone here!"

And then it hits me—the power of community and improvisation. "We'll wing it!" I say. "Let's invent Casa Grande's first annual Christmas potluck."

It takes a bit of explaining, especially to the Norwegian couple who'd never heard of the concept, much less the word "potluck." The rest just have to come to terms with the fact there was no going out to some nice restaurant and that no matter what they brought, it'd be fine. They had a whole day to figure it out and procure something. *Anything, frankly.*

Christmas in Puerto Rico isn't a two-day event like in the States. Instead it's the "twelve days of Christmas," like in the song, and it's called Three Kings' Days. Puerto Ricans are known for taking their merrymaking pretty seriously. Bales, the island's largest hardware store and lumberyard, closes from Christmas Eve to January 6. Try running an inn in the tropics and not needing to repair something for twelve days. The year before we'd gotten smart and went in the day before to stock up on things we might need. This time it's too late; the hardware store is closing early to get ready for the days off ahead. Believe me, I have nothing but admiration for their priorities in this regard.

Anyway, the Norwegians are busy figuring out if they can get ingredients for meatballs at Super Descuento Morales before the store closes. The chef from Quebec scores fresh yellowtail fish at the *pescadería*. The dramatic screenplay author from Denver and her daughter opt to make a sweet potato casserole, while the food writer from North Carolina outsmarts us all and makes a local version of green papaya salad, using up the abundance we have on the property. That inspires Bill to harvest bananas from the property to grill with chunks of fresh coconut, served up with rum, ordinary vanilla ice cream, and squeeze-bottle chocolate sauce. *Si perfecto! Buen provecho!*

Like all large meals at the big house, our Christmas dinner is on the deck. It's the only dining room we have, so the palm fronds, the frogs, the crickets, and the stars are a part of it. Most likely Cesária Évora or the Buena Vista Social Club is playing, as my favorite iPod playlist, Fiesta La Finca, has more than four hours of dinner-on-the-deck classics. Our table, an old piece of plywood, seats twelve to fourteen with no problem. Our centerpiece is a collection of candle lanterns with favorite shells and plant cuttings in old jars, somehow elegantly arranged. Maybe you have to squint or tilt your head in a certain way to see it, but we all see it and feel it. There is elegance in the funk and coziness of a room with no walls.

The evening is more than the "fine" I'd promised. It is great. These dozen people, from various generations, countries, and states, couples, families, solo travelers, straight, gay, well-seasoned globetrotters, and first-timers, have spent the afternoon working around each other in the main house's large guest kitchen. Now they are sharing a meal—a holiday—laughing it up and swapping stories around the table. It turns out Lars, the young Norwegian guy, is leaving the next day to crew on a massive, square-rigged tall ship for a multi-month transatlantic crossing. The mother and daughter confess that this is their first time traveling together in years and they are trying to feel comfortable with each other.

This is the magic of La Finca: Strangers become friends, catastrophes become comedies. Dinner becomes a charade game that morphs into folks playing music on the deck. I don't remember if we dance that night—we usually do—under the inky-black star-studded sky. At the end, over the dishes, the shy young gay woman from Room 5, who's been reticent about joining the festivities and nervous about what to bring, says quietly, without even turning to me, "I think that was the best Christmas I've ever had."

From then on, finca potlucks become an institution. Who knew so many chefs, restaurateurs, caterers, food writers, and such made up a large percentage of our guest pool? Bill and I are usually too tired to cook after our long days and burned out on the relatively limited Vieques grocery selections, so hosting and dining with serious foodies serves us well. And now that we are really on the island full time, we get to know the farmers and best local sources for fish, meat, and produce. We make friends with them, and our island life gets richer.

We branch out. We invite the guests from the cabins and our friends from the island to join forces and share food. Weird coincidences, what we call finca magic, pop up—like one dinner party where we had three physicists, each from a different group of guests; another where it's all families with teens; and another with three alums from the same university sitting at the table with their current dean of students. We arrange a finca-wide happy hour on the deck one evening for no real reason at all, only to discover that every last one of the attendees—over twenty people—is from Brooklyn. Some of them are still friends today.

During ordinary days the pace and extent of the work is profound. The day-in, day-out relentlessness is unmatched in my career or Bill's. No wonder so many managers have fried out. If you didn't own the place, it would be difficult to imagine wanting to work this hard for long. We haven't been to the beach in weeks. Two times in six weeks, all told. This is nuts. Aren't the beaches what it's all about? I'm way too tired to figure it out—one more thing to put on the to-do list.

Thank God for the slow season, or, in our case, the lambing season, which pulls us back to the Northwest. We can always relax back in our other life in Washington, in a small homestead we call Little Hill. Back in the States we have migrated from city life to the country, from the rat race to bottle-feeding lambs, mucking stalls, and putting in spring garden beds. We are officially retired; really, we've just exchanged our paying jobs to a nonpaying form of work. It's hard, but it's nothing like life at La Finca. On Vieques there are days when I can't find time to catch my breath or brush my teeth. If I am able to finish my coffee in the morning, that's a good start, possibly an omen that things that day are relatively under control. At least for the moment.

The finca tends to blur the lines between work and play, friends and guests, indoors and out, normal and not so much, and private and public. We are okay with that. Heck, we set it up that way. We've put the office in our cabin's main living room. That means for early morning check-out guests might find me still in my muumuu. Most mornings, though, as soon as the coffee is done we move our essential office things—the massive, all-important reservation calendar that tells us who's checking in and out, the iPad, my daily to-do list—to our cabin's deck, the same place where we crash on the couch in the evening. But now, with the mockingbird's wake-up call, the hummingbirds darting this way and that on their missions, while it is still shady and soft in the morning light, it is our office workspace.

My desk is two two-by-six boards that Bill has laid across the corner rail of the deck to hold his old sink planter. Nothing very elegant, but it works great. No need to nail anything down; the sink is heavy enough to hold it all in place. This way I can keep a close eye on my seedlings and plant starters. And because it's just off of the main house deck, I can keep half an ear out for anyone who needs anything up there. I'm not spying on them, but I am closer than the guests probably know. I'm hidden by an enormous waxy philodendron, at least twenty-five feet of it, that wraps around and weaves into the tree between the two buildings. I don't mean to hide; I just do, like a bird camouflaged in the foliage. And being on the southeast, windward corner, my little rail desk catches the breeze. My office without walls.

It's no coincidence that there are no boundaries, either. People come at all hours looking for all sorts of things. A little kid can wander up quietly and ask in a tiny voice, "I read on your blog you have a frog who lives in your sink. Can I see it?" (Which I love.) Or "Did I hear you have a way of making espresso by hand in here? The three of us in Casa Nueva would just love—" (Which I don't always love.) Steps on the wooden walkway—I can hear them coming. A smiling face peeks around the corner.

Usually it's just folks wanting to be pointed to the right beach or restaurant or wanting more information on the bio-bay. Our guests aren't the public, a random sampling of folks. They are the kind of people who choose a place like La Finca. That in itself means they are for the most part different or somehow quirky, easygoing at the very least, and always interesting.

Here's the funny part. Even if I'm deep into a project that needs my full attention, I don't mind the interruption. They aren't just our customers, and they aren't just nice. They feel like friends. Bill and I both sort of fall in love with them: the little kids who come down from the family cabaña with a note asking for candles and end up sitting there with Bill showing them how banana blossoms turn into bunches. Or the professor looking for directions who ends up staying for half an hour to teach us about the difference between the civil codes and legal systems in Puerto Rico and the United States. From the environmental economist from Switzerland's UN delegation, whose real love is his part-time job of piloting helicopter tours over Manhattan, to the prominent Italian journalist who wants to know if it's easy to buy dope on the island, they are all fascinating.

Being their innkeeper is like being a mom. It wears you out. But it's not like you're going to stop. You can't. As with a toddler, all needs seem immediate. Guests need questions answered or help with something that rightfully can't wait. So what if my coffee gets cold? The cabaña toilet needs fixing, the propane in the casita needs to be reordered, the pool needs a tarantula removed, the icemaker in the fridge needs tweaking. On my way to that, I make a mental note that we really should pick the mangoes before any more fall to the ground. They are littering the lawn, and there's a whiff of sweet, rotting fruit in the air.

There's also a large looming dark cloud to the south, and the laundry on the line is dry, so that needs taking down ASAP. Just as I start to grab the sheets off the line, two seven-year-old girls come running up with one more question. I think I may lose it completely, but before I do one bashfully asks, "Can we help you fold the laundry? We like how pretty the sheets and colors look blowing around."

Her cousin adds, "I never saw laundry dry outside before. Can you teach us how to use clothespins?"

Now that we are in the saddle at least for a good chunk of the year, we have learned firsthand what works and what doesn't. We know what skill sets are needed—and it's a crazy, long, wide range of skills—and how to find the folks with the experience, temperament, and wherewithal.. How perfect that after more months of searching the horizons, we find sailors to take charge of this boat. Even our kids approve of these two.

Pam and Graham sail in from Florida to start their life dream of moving to the Caribbean to blend retirement from the corporate world with sailing and work. They won't be here forever, but they promise us two great years, and they deliver. *Boom.* The place is run ship-shape. They know the tropics. They know what they're doing, and they do it well. Graham can fix and build anything that's needed. Pam is equally comfortable playing hostess, housekeeper, seamstress, and costrategist over the phone with me on group reservations and everything else. They understand the need for small footprints and sustainability and know how to work a computer. We have folks at the helm that can take it and run.

Once things begin to run smoothly, I can see how much I love not only the guests but the physical spaces of La Finca. I have favorite places tucked here and there, benches or the hammocks I choose depending on the time of day, and favorite vistas, either wide views or blooming plants, depending on the season. I've always had places and corners I love for certain reasons, like the big windows in the main house kitchen, where the lizards do their push-ups against the glass in the mornings, sometimes opposite a cousin or mate, I don't know. Often some identical lizard follows suit, in the exact spot on the window but outside, so the two form a mirror image, pushing in and out in sync. Some sort of lizard fantasy sex game or battle? I have no idea, but it's a regular part of cooking breakfast in the main house kitchen.

Another favorite time and place match has been the front porch, just off the laundry area. There's a hammock most folks scurry by en route to the showers or the pool, just down the path. But if you take a minute in the late afternoon to stop and swing, you can watch the hummingbirds come sip the nectar of the purple banana blossom. Just before it closes up for the night, the petal arches up and opens fully. The emerald hummers duck in and out and hover for as long as they can, before night falls and the petals close up or drop to the ground.

I love the intersection of built and natural spaces. Some we inherited, others we created. Maybe it was growing up in Northern California's mild climate. As a child I liked to play architect and sketch up dream houses. The persistent goal was making a house where you couldn't tell inside from outside. It's like that at La Finca. The climate defines our interior spaces and usually minimizes our time in them. Buildings have to be right, and they have to be simple.

Hot afternoon. I take a break to write and see my face reflected in the screen. I see a lot more wrinkles than were there 15 years ago. I'm so much happier now, with them, than I was without. And although there may not be a direct correlation, I draw my own. My wrinkles give me certain privileges, like my graying hair does. I get to say and do things with a certain developing "old lady license." Adding eccentric innkeeper to the mix just gives me that much more freedom. But then — la finca has always done that for me.

Just like it lets me paint my murals — with not quite reckless abandon, but more and more every year. Just like it lets me dance on the beach, early in the morning, when I used to just walk.

I particularly love the built spaces we've scattered across the property. It's not that they don't drive me crazy with missed opportunities. Bill and I were both well aware that we should have used a different piling here or a wider board there, or a different kind of wood, and how much better it would have been if I had stopped before going overboard with that paint or done a more careful job. Those are two core lifelong traits, and though La Finca is full of evidence of both, I've learned not to get too bothered by any of it. Breathe deep, again, and practice total acceptance.

I see the powerful effect space has on moods and actions, so it's fun to create them together. For the most part Bill is responsible for building and maintaining the cabins, and I furnish and equip them, all on our shoestring budget. It's not just to save money. Early Garage Sale is more than a fashion statement, more than a reduce-reuse-recycle way of life. Besides being good for the planet, our practice of using mismatched sheets and towels, chipped plates, and faded throw pillows is about providing the unexpected, tossing a little whimsy into our guests' vacations. They see immediately that they can let their hair and guard down. No one is trying to look perfect here. There is something about the honesty and history of well-worn things that helps people relax. Maybe La Finca is the Velveteen Rabbit of guesthouses.

How perfect that I should marry an architect. Neither Bill nor I want to take away anything from this sweet corner of the natural world by overbuilding on her. We probably already have, but we try to go gently and carefully. We both smile and nod when friends and guests offer their long and varied suggestions about what we could do to the place.

Either we're getting old and tiring of the endless projects or, in our old-age wisdom, finally figuring out that less is truly more. Good enough is just that.

REED
BDAY → 50!

23

ikebana/vase

ROOTS, ROAST
& REGGAE
for 12

QUANTII	PRICE EACH
t to 375°	1.75

in olive oil
rinated pork shoulder chunks
green sofrito
6-8 whole garlic
1 3" piece of fresh ginger root
2 onions cut into chunks
1 or 2 green or red, Anaheim or
poblano peppers
Any combination of root vegetables
cut into large chunks: Potatoes,
yams, carrots, parsnips, yellow
beets, yucca.
2 green (half ripe) plantains cut
into 3/4" slices.
1 cup of white wine
salt and pepper to taste
4 cans of coconut milk

Roast 2 hours in a large Dutch
Oven.

Call it good

ASS

TEA. TOWEL

CHELSEA + BEN
to 4118

PRINT SHOW? —6PM
DINNER? Albe

TEXT
CHAR

best to think of grocery shopping as an adventure

Don't Stop The Canary

a new novel by

casera FRIJOLES

casera HABICHUELAS NEGRAS

and learn to be happy with what you discover

19.

When Alice Comes to Visit

Because of Pam and Graham and the ship-shapeness of it all, the following year our winter stint is easier to slip into. We have our routines and rituals down, and we have some idea of what to expect (i.e., the unexpected). We're all set. Our arrival allows Pam and Graham to sail south through the Windward Islands for the months we'll be on La Finca's deck. By mid-January the season seems to be flowing, going off without a hitch. It's fun to see the familiar faces of returning guests from last year: the Sierra Club, the marine ecology department from the University of Massachusetts. They know the ropes as well, so it's smooth sailing all around. Even the first-time guests are more comfortable. Or maybe it's us. It's almost like we're getting the hang of it. We strike a rare, fragile balance of work and play.

"Sweet!" Gus says on the phone, in his snowboarder kind of way, when I have to report in to my kids, who are worried we will work as hard this year as we did last year. "Really, Mom, I'm glad to hear it."

To them, life on Vieques is all about the beach. They, like most visitors, measure the success of their trip by time in the water—swimming, snorkeling, diving, fishing. Me, I'm not so sure that's my yardstick of success. But even by their standards I'm doing okay. I'm swimming in the pool almost every afternoon. Guests are gone then, so I have it to myself both to relax and to exercise. Bill is drawing and playing the guitar a lot. And vital sign or not, we are actually getting ourselves to the beach, often enough that we even lose count. The year before it was twice in the first two months we were there.

"This is great. I could go on like this for a long time," Bill says as we look over the calendar.

"Do you think these open few weeks ahead are a problem?" I ask. Seems like I worry more than he does about the business side of things.

"Who cares if they are? Why sweat it? Let's just enjoy the place." Bill is more confident and casual about it all. Friends have been telling me the same thing for years. And fewer guests do mean less work.

"You're right. We could kick back." Bill gets back to his evening guitar. I have the time and energy to cook a good dinner.

The next day Anne calls—Anne, our friend and silent partner, the one who saved me from losing the place. "Alice is coming," she states, as if that were normal news.

Anne owns two successful restaurants in Manhattan. She started them from scratch and has built them into New York institutions—no small feat for someone who started as a young wannabe chef from northern California. Before New York she was sous chef for Alice Waters at Chez Panisse, what was then Alice's innovative French restaurant in Berkeley, half a block from where my family had lived. No surprise, the two of them became lifelong friends.

I wonder if either had any idea then that this sweet little restaurant would become the legendary home of what was first called California Cuisine and is now considered by many to be the birthplace of North America's slow and local food movement, or that Alice would accomplish all she has with food for schools and the public's food consciousness. Six months later, after this call, Time magazine includes her as one of the hundred most important people in the world.

I know her better as Anne's good friend. I've met her a few times, on those few lucky evenings when I was able to dine at Chez, as my sister Jane calls it. She knew Alice too, of course. They both share best-friend status with Anne. Jane lived a block away and had helped with Alice's foundation and its Edible Schoolyard Project. So naturally Alice stopped by the table to say hi to Anne or Jane.

"That's great. When are you guys thinking?" I say, assuming they will come together. I look at the open month ahead on the reservation calendar.

"That's just it. She wants to come with a friend at the end of January, when I'm going to be in Bali."

"Huh?" I say. I go sort of blank. I see a vision of Alice from many years before. We were all preparing for Anne's fiftieth birthday party when suddenly Alice walked in, pointed to some potted palms in the hall of our golf course venue, and decisively said, "Those have got to go." Don't get me wrong. She wasn't mean or nasty, or commanding or in any way wrong, or negative. She was just clear. She knows what she thinks is right. And she cares a great deal about that rightness. I have read a few recipes, enough to know about that clarity and sureness—two things I don't always have. I stumble along, and I have a good time doing it.

But now, suddenly, we're hosting one of the nation's leading hostesses—in two weeks?

Anyone I know who knows food and likes to cook almost worships Alice Waters. "Worships" is their word, not mine. But I have always tended to scorn celebs. And as soon as I know someone or something is in or groovy, I veer the other way. I vote under-dog. I prefer the undiscovered holes-in-the-wall to the legendary places with long lines of folks waiting to get in. I'm sure I get that from my mother.

I know Alice's work and her realm, and it goes way beyond cooking. She's about graciousness. Community. Sustainability. Quality. Style. Authenticity. Hospitality. All intimate but at the same time on a grand scale—or world stage. And all, seemingly, sort of perfect. She's legendary. Opinionated. Important. And she's coming to stay with me. Funky, irreverent me, who's never used the autographed cookbook of hers that Jane gave me. Me, who buys cheap wine and goat cheese from Trader Joe's. Here in our plywood cabins and the hodgepodge of thrift store finds, Ikea bargains, and New Dawn two-by-four lumber furniture. We're hosting *Alice Waters?* On our own?

Anne is still talking when I regain consciousness. "Yep, I know it's a drag. I've always wanted to show her the place myself, but she'll be in DC right before that and she just really needs a place to relax for a week." Anne sounds serious, like this isn't a joke. For her, it wouldn't be a joke or even a big deal. She travels in that world and shares that kind of confidence. "Is Casa Nueva available?" she adds. "I think she'd like that best."

My anxiety is swirled up with my fear of being judged. I do things in my own odd-ball way, and it works—at least for me, Bill, the guests, and our kids. At least most of the time. I'm not usually very interested when folks start telling me what *Condé Nast Traveler* or *Travel and Leisure* would think of the way we do such-and-such. Or that we'd be docked a notch for this or that on the official bed-and-breakfast rating system. I don't care. Wanting their approval would imply they have some authority or at least relevance, and they don't. Sure, I love that the *New York Times* has featured us and that *Lonely Planet* calls us the "personification of Vieques." But they love us for what we are, for the way we do our own thing. Call it funky, rustic, offbeat. I don't want to hear about a standard that means nothing to me. But here I am, tied up in knots with worry about being judged.

Sadly, the only thing free for that whole week is the family cabaña, a lovable but sort of goofy tall plywood cabin built by the women of New Dawn. For some reason it's almost perpetually in need of attention, if not some major repair or another, and it's regularly overtaken by the mango tree, bougainvillea, or ginger around it. In the cabaña, "floor plan" is an oxymoron. Over the years we have made many improve-ments, starting by replacing the ladder with a stairway and putting a bathroom door where there hadn't been one, ripping out the built-in double bed, and redoing the entire upstairs so that a full queen bed fits. It has a new porch, new deck, new shower, and new kitchen counters, and this year we planned on new kitchen windows and shutters.

I laugh when people call it funky. "You should have seen it when . . ." I say. Luckily the folks who stay there love it, and love is at least farsighted. Let's pray the magic works for Alice, because that's all we have for her.

"Hey, Bill!" I call out to him—or maybe the universe—when I get off the phone. I'm hoping either he or the fates can swoop in and take care of this. But he is out doing his regular afternoon raking of the rubber leaves.

I look around my shabby little manager cabin / living room office, with its milk crate desk organizer; the cartoony island tourist map, with pink-highlighted routes that I've taped to the desktop; the rusted-shut file cabinet; the "project shelves" I've hidden by stapling up an old sheet. All pretty makeshift. True, it's all comfortable, but suddenly it looks so tacky.

What will Alice think of it? What will she think of any of this? How will the softness of our Goodwill cotton sheets compare with fine French linen? Our mismatched dishes don't quite qualify as shabby chic. Would she dare to cook in our old enamel pans? How about the scratched Teflon frying pans? How much can we replace? Would that be dishonest, somehow disingenuous? Would Alice understand how hard things are to get here? Or how hard it is to keep knives sharpened? Oh, God, our knives! As usual they are in a hopeless state. Do we have enough time to get an order delivered from the main island?

The highest-quality grade of almost anything for us is good old Costco, from meats and cheese to bread and knives. And for anyone on Vieques, it takes a week or so from the time you place an order for it to arrive at your home, assuming it arrives at all. Getting on and off the island with a vehicle is such a hassle with the ferry system that only a few folks go over regularly to make pickup runs. They charge you a percentage of the purchase price. So the savings you get from shopping at Costco or any other big box store evaporates.

But that's okay. At least you found the gluten-free rice crackers the Sierra Club is counting on for their group. Oh, but maybe you didn't. Maybe they are out of stock at the store, the delivery guy ran out of time or space on the truck, or the ferry was over-loaded. Maybe the cooler wasn't cool, so the spinach the yoga group ordered cooked itself on the way home. Or your shopper didn't know what you meant by Earl Grey tea or an "everything" bagel. I had to explain to one family why they had Pillsbury crescent rolls rather than the croissants they had ordered. I'm looking at the number of days between this minute and Alice's arrival. My head is spinning.

It's a good thing Bill doesn't hear me thinking. Or maybe he does and knows I need to calm down before I drown him in my own chaos. When he finally comes in and hears the news, even he gulps, and then we get to work. First, a list of what we need to do to the cabaña: cleaning, painting, ordering new sharp knives and coarse salt grinders, at the very least.

"Being Alice-ready" becomes our slogan and total focus. In truth, it was all stuff we needed to do anyway, but now we are motivated, moving at speeds not often seen on the island. I didn't need Martha Stewart to tell me that the scratched-up smiling sunshine painted floor "rug" that Xing and I had done way back when just would not do. And then there were those ugly chipboard and plastic bedside tables in the cabaña's extra kids' bedroom. I never knew where they came from and had hated them since they arrived. It was time to purge, or at least move them to the manager's cabin.

My mother had passed away about six months earlier. I was just beginning to embrace the mantle of her legacy. Mom had only been to the finca once, many years before, and she was less than enthusiastic about it. Regardless, she is somehow around now. For most of my adult life, all of us had teased Mom for her over-the-top thriftiness and beyond-the-pale environmental determination. With her death and the sorting of her things and the memories that entailed, I became conscious in a new way of our closeness and our deep similarities. For inexplicable reasons, it wasn't until after she was gone that I felt okay with admitting just how much of her values and resulting goofy behavior matched my own.

I didn't start saving jar lids and plastic yogurt tubs by the dozen—I had my limits, and other foibles—but I noticed that, like Mom, I cut tea towels in half to make two or saved the perfectly good section of an old favorite sheet to make dishcloths or rags. I didn't mind if people thought I was a weirdo. I figured it was worth it: good for kids to see how easy it is to leave a smaller footprint, even if they were tiny steps. Just the awareness of the effort was a good thing. Not in a preachy way, just in a doing sort of way.

But Mom was also a narcissist and judgmental as all get-out. Everything we did was held up to her high standard and was rarely up to par. I have both inherited and worked hard to offload that part of her legacy. Between her and being the youngest of four in a busy family of outspoken siblings, feeling seen was a treat, and feeling respected—evaluated in a positive light—even rarer. Maybe I feel more confident now because no one from my past is weighing my merits.

But conflicting feelings of caring and not caring, being clear and then muddled, aren't helping me get things done. And that's all I need to worry about now. With Alice's visit less than a week away, I have to get her cabin ready, starting with that ugly painted rug.

What was Chief Dan George's last line in *Little Big Man*?

"Sometimes the magic works...

...and sometimes it doesn't."

I am sitting on the cabaña floor covered in paint spatters and sweat. The afternoon sun is pouring in, and it's hot. The oscillating fan helps, even though it often gets stuck pointing to the far left. I'm too hassled to run down to the main house and see if I can find a better one. Besides, the clicking sound and the swoosh of the fan as it crosses the room has a kind of rhythm to it. I just want this to be done—and to look good. But my paint "combing" technique, where I drag and scrape one paint color across another with a rubber squeegee, is not working. The rubber edge is too brittle from the climate. There's no telling if I'll be able to find another squeegee on the island, so, ugh, it's a mess, or worse. This odd fleshy beige I've concocted is not the deep terra cotta I am trying to get.

Does anything work around here? Between the heat and the blowing air, the unscratched flesh paint is drying in thick, drippy lines across the floor. At least our old smiley-face sun is gone. "Alice-ready. Must be Alice-ready. Must not get hassled," I'm chanting mindlessly to myself. It isn't working. Even Bill doesn't have a clue what to do with the new barf-textured floor when he stops by. Time is running out, and he has his own projects to deal with, so he's off to the pool. I'm there on my own, with my odd colors and textures, when a small miracle happens.

My guardian angel, whom I've met only a few times before, flies in the open porch window, as if riding in on a trade wind. She flutters through the fanning hot air, lands on my shoulder, and gently whacks me a good one with her small wand. I've found that with angel messages it is not so much the words as the magic behind the tiny thud that carries the weight. Practice what you preach! The impact resonates from its pinprick. After she gets my attention with that, she's a little gentler: *Calming way down now and staying calm is the only answer. If you get flustered and nervous now, when Alice is here you—we—are absolutely hosed. We are, tacky or not, who we are. Your only chance is to be your honest, albeit makeshift, self. Her restaurant, her work, has always been real, and about being real. We are real too, just maybe a funkier version of it. Just be your best, most creative, truest self.* And then she is gone.

The icky beige suddenly looks better, a more interesting earthy brown. I cut a few fresh notches into the dried-out rubber squeegee, drag the new red across the bumps, and *voilà*! There it is! That long-sought-after level of "good enough" is just fine.

Having found my mindful, grounded self helps my outlook. I notice that the overgrown hibiscus is in bloom and a handful of redbuds are pressing against the window screen. They'll be blooming, forming a beautiful natural curtain, when Alice arrives in a few days. In my new collectedness, I call the friend of Alice's who is coming with her and helping arrange their travel.

I'm breathing; I'm cool with this. "Hey, there," I say, casual and comfortable. "Just wanted to check in and make sure you're all set with traveling down, and if there is anything you guys would like to have on hand when you arrive. I'm happy to pick up things at the store."

"Oh, that's a great idea," her friend says. "We'd love that. How about I email you a list?"

I am starting to feel okay about this whole thing when the email comes in:

"Homemade tortillas, any local goat cheese, fresh local salsa, any local veggies and fruit." Nothing here is extraordinary or any different from my own lists—at home. On Vieques it's a whole other thing. It's clear that these dear guests, like most, have no idea how remote the island is. Was it Hemingway who said that only in the Caribbean could people open a can of peas and call it a salad? How do I graciously reset their expectations from fresh, local, and homemade to whatever we can find?

There aren't any goat cheeses to choose from on the island. There are a few goat farms, but they are small family concerns; sadly, no dairies. (There used to be. Our gardener Miguel tells me how he and his mom used to make cheese on their farm, years ago, when Puerto Rico was primarily agricultural.) Nowadays there's no guarantee you'll find even Kraft cheddar in our largest store. Puerto Ricans don't cook much with salsa or tortillas, so fresh or homemade versions are virtually unheard of. We are happy when our Super Descuento Morales has plain Doritos. Tostitos salsa isn't half bad if you add a lot of our mangoes and recao. And, well, the whole produce situation is always a challenge. You never know what you'll find. Most fruits and vegetables in the store come from California, and, like any traveler from that far away, it's pretty worn out by the time it arrives.

The next day we welcome new guests, a couple of Sylvia's friends from San Juan. As they head off to their room, she exclaims, "Oh, I almost forgot! Sylvia asked me to give you this, *con besos y gracias*." She gives me big grin and hands me a large woven plastic shopping bag. The bag itself is cool enough as a gift, but knowing Sylvia it will be filled with treasures, some new pillowslips or one of her handmade dreamcatchers. But it's a bag of groceries, all fresh, local, and homemade. I am incredulous. First of all, I had no idea these things were available, even in San Juan. Second, I hadn't even talked to Sylvia. How could she have known about Alice's visit or her shopping wish list? Yet somehow here are the exact things Alice had asked for. I look at her without speaking. I'm not able to. It's too weird. I look around for any signs of my angel.

"They are all from the neighborhood farmers market in Ocean Park."

I'm still unable to process how this could have happened. I look at Bill; did he talk to Sylvia? The gal must have read my mind, just as Sylvia apparently had done. "She told me she knows the sorts of things you like, and she knows you can't get very much over here."

She pulls out a bag of soft homemade tortillas, a chunk of a local cheese, a tub of fresh salsa, and an array of beautiful, odd-shaped, exotic tropical fruits and vegetables. "I think they are all from Puerto Rico. You know Sylvia, she really cares about all that."

It's going to be one of those things I will never be able to figure out. Regardless, I head to the cabaña to stock the fridge and make a welcome fruit bowl out of these wondrous things. I have to confess to more than a pang of envy as I unpack the bag into what will become Alice's kitchen for the coming week. These are treats we haven't had in months and truly covet. But this coincidence is too magical not to share. *This is what they mean by sharing the love.*

We manage to get a new set of knives and a coarse salt grinder, two things I know Alice will want. She won't have to deal with the clogged-up salt shakers, wet and thick with humidity despite the rice we add, which never seems to work. So this is progress. And after sweating over various combinations, I've gotten her room upstairs looking good. I've settled on some favorite lime green vintage hula-girl pillowcases, some soft striped pink sheets, and an orange bedspread. Playing with our linen colors is just part of our corporate protocol. That and adding a bunch of fresh cuttings to the jar on the desk.

Getting things ready—the fixing, cleaning, painting, hanging, and rehanging of artwork, the snipping and primping while staying real and calm—is exhausting stuff. Finally the cabaña is as ready as it will be, and lo and behold, here we are at the gate, exhausted, honest us. Breathing, staying grounded, and welcoming them.

She is friendly and excited to be here, oohing and ahhing over the grounds and views as we walk to the cabaña. As soon as she sees the cornucopia of fruits on the counter, Alice is fondling the bumpy and the beautiful. I added some of our own coconuts, large hard, green plantains, and tiny yellow bananas. She loves it all and asks questions about everything as she begins to unpack a few things. First she carefully unrolls a soft travel case. Slowly, one by one, she reveals a set of knives. Ha! Then a large bag of something seemingly precious and heavy. She pulls it out of its protective wrapping, a bag of chunky, very coarse salt; next, a small mortar and pestle. She not only brings her own, but grinds it, by hand. Hard not to chuckle at our Kirkland brand salt grinder and new knives right behind her. Oh, well, that family over in Casa Nueva will love the upgrades. As subtly as I can, I slip them into my apron pockets.

Sitting on the deck a bit later, they go over some of the things they hope to do during the week, like snorkeling. "I know I'll be fine, but I'm a little nervous about it. I just have to jump in. You know what I mean?" Alice says.

"Oh, I do," I say, and laugh. "I know exactly how you feel. I'm feeling that way right now, at this moment. I want to do something, but I'm a little scared."

They look confused.

I breathe, and then I just jump in. "Would you like to come to dinner? We're just grilling up some churrasco, nothing fancy. But I guess that sort of goes without saying."

They laugh. Alice seems delighted.

I am breathing deep again as I wander back to my place. It looks like I'm cooking for Alice Waters. Better get to work. Gulp.

Just like my tiny angel predicted, it all goes fine. The meal is okay. Not my best, frankly, but it doesn't matter. How wrong can you go with ceviche, grilled steak, and rice and beans? The palms, the view, the temperature of the evening work its charm. Besides, we are too busy talking about Alice's recent trip to China with Yo-Yo Ma and Meryl Streep. The food doesn't matter.

As we do with all our guests, Bill and I balance our helpfulness with staying out of the way. We know how rare a real week off is for Alice, so we tell no one, not even best friends, not even guests in the other houses, that she is here. Protecting her from the fanfare is a treasured gift, easy for us to give. A few days into her stay we invite her to a potluck on the main house deck. Guests and friends are grilling and eating with her, yucking it up without a clue who she is. Perfect.

They take us up on an offer to tour our friend Jorge's amazing farm and is appropriately amazed by his handiwork in the garden and the traditional Puerto Rican woodcarving he learned from his father. He has things for sale inside his tiny open-air house—more like a beach shelter than a house in the American sense of the word. The wood smoke from the stove is strong, and mixed with drying herbs from the garden it makes for a thick and delicious, almost savory air. Alice covets a small wooden spatula she finds near Jorge's large open-fire cookstove. The smooth wood and shape of the spatula feels good in her hand.

"I love this. How much?" Alice asks.

"*Lo siento*," Jorge says. He speaks only Spanish. He goes on to explain that this one is his favorite; he uses it, so it's not for sale. He doesn't have a clue who this woman is, other than a friend of ours, although he probably wouldn't have done anything differently if he did. He tries to get Alice interested in some new ones, but she explains that this spatula is special, with the perfect balance and form in her hand. He smiles, but no. They reach an impasse, but it's clear they each respect the other for their mutual admiration of the small simple tool. All good—we go on our way.

A few days later Alice invites Bill and me up to their cabaña for dinner. To say it's great sounds stupid—of course it's great. But as fabulous as the food is, the real treat is the opportunity to watch the slow, easy way everything is prepared. Everything chopped, ground, by hand. The shrimp and the rustic, chunky sauce, what she calls "finca-style pesto," is by far the best either of us has ever had.

The highlight of the evening comes when we sit at the table and I see her napkins. Here I am, a crazy lady who insists on everyone at La Finca using cloth napkins. Another one of our corporate protocols, I guess. In every house we proudly supply a handful of colorful thrift store options: sweet flowers from the '60s, weird geometric designs from the '70s, tasteful mauve from the '80s, and so on. Unfortunately there's more polyester than I'd like, but that's the way things go. House policy asks that each finca guest takes one, bonds with it, and uses it for their stay. We have napkin rings to help distinguish them. I take a fair amount of teasing for being a touch too frugal and quirky from friends and family but not from many guests; they are too polite. I really don't care. It's worth it to reduce the island's solid waste issue and to get people thinking about how easy it is to do things differently.

But the table is set without any of our napkins. Instead each of us has a dishcloth, actually half a dishcloth, folded at our place setting. I see that its cut edge is raw from being ripped in half. Alice sees my intrigue and explains that from all the traveling she's done, it's just become a habit of hers. Like me, she likes cloth napkins and has seen the cotton ones get harder to find. Like me, she hates to waste things.

Alice's "Finca Pasta"
From *The Art of Simple Food*

Pounded Almond & Mint Pasta Sauce
4 servings (about 1 1/2 cups)

This is an improvisation on basil pesto. I call it La
Finca pasta, as I made it on a farm in Puerto Rico
where there was lots of mint and no basil or
Parmesan cheese. Mint, almonds, and garlic are
pounded together with a touch of tomato for balance.

Peel, seed, and dice:
    1 small tomato
Blanch for 20 seconds in boiling water:
    1/2 cup almonds
Drain, cool, and slip off the skins.
Using a mortar and pestle, pound to a paste:
    2 medium garlic cloves
    A pinch of salt
Add the almonds a handful at a time, pounding all
the while. Add the diced tomato and pound into the
almonds. Remove the nut mixture from the mortar.
Chop:
    3 cups mint leaves
Add the chopped leaves to the mortar with:
    A large pinch of salt
Pound the leaves to a paste. Return the pounded
almond mixture to the mortar. Pound the mint and
almond mixture together. Continue pounding as
you gradually pour in:
    1/4 cup extra-virgin olive oil
Taste for salt and adjust as needed. Toss the sauce
with cooked pasta and a few tablespoons pasta cooking water. Finish the pasta with a drizzle of:
    Extra-virgin olive oil

BUEN PROVECHO!

"Dishcloths are perfect. They are better
made and still cotton. But they are too big to use
for one each," Alice says. "I just tear them into
the right size and voila! I'll leave them for you, if
you like. Seems like a finca sort of thing."

I don't know if I felt it happen right at that
moment, but looking back it's clear that this
was when a newfound confidence begins to
bloom inside me. I was in my midfifties, ready
to reach crone stage; I must have been ready.
Little haunting negative internal voices got
quieter. Suddenly I was no longer the crazy
old lady who does this sort of thing, the weird
little sister who is too much like Mom for her
own good, the way-too-frugal ex-wife. I was
just me. And goofy eccentric me is okay, in
fact, more than okay, by the standards and heroes others live by and worship.

Before Alice, I figured I pretty much knew
what we were in for with her visit. But I didn't
have a clue. The biggest surprise wasn't how
relaxed and easy it was to have her. The
shocker was that I had no idea her stay would
become one of my life's little milestones.

"It's perfect," Alice says to me one night,
when I apologize in case I've overstepped my
bounds with advice on how to dress for kayaking on the bio-bay. She takes both my hands
and looks up at me. "You, and all of this, this
whole place, it's all just perfect. It's clear you
know what you're doing, and you are having so
much fun doing it. That's marvelous."

"Little milestone?" Who am I kidding?—
that was a life-changing moment. Although I
had no idea at the time.

I remember, as a very young girl, standing
in front of a full-length mirror in a hallway.
Jane asked what I was doing. When I respond-
ed that I was just looking, she warned me
that I better not; I might become conceited.

It sounded serious, like an illness, a condition you could catch from the mirror. I asked her what she meant.

"It's what happens when you think you're cute," Jane said.

Maybe I'd been caught daydreaming in front of my reflection on numerous occasions, or singing "I Feel Pretty" from our *West Side Story* album one too many times. I don't know if it's one memory of many such warnings or if it's just the loving guidance of an older sister who understandably didn't want me to be like Mom, in what we now recognize as that narcissistic way of hers.

Something certainly must have caught hold, lodging itself in my core for the next five decades or so. As talkative as I am and as confident as I may appear, the truth is that I am equally afraid of appearing self-centered or self-absorbed, conceited or narcissistic, you name it. When you grow up with it, it's hard to know any different. I never knew exactly what schoolmates meant when they called me a show-off. What was I showing off? Or what could I do to change their minds? If you dance down the beach or raise your hand in class or play the court jester, are you showing off or just being yourself? I learned to keep a lot of things to myself—and certainly wouldn't take ownership of any creative effort.

Though I used creativity throughout my career as a writer, designer, and creative director—and later to build La Finca—I never considered myself a creative person. I shrugged off any achievement by acknowledging my luck, the team, the timing, saying, "The stars must have aligned." All of which is true, of course—but I couldn't see my own worth.

Something, somehow, in Alice Waters's crazy, unexpected acknowledgment allowed me to feel an enormous validation that started a shift in how I saw myself. It didn't end there, but it started. The old power of positive thinking. Encouragement. I've heard it all a thousand times. Who knew it worked at this age? And once that shift takes place you are on a new path. Even if it's barely off that other well-beaten, rutted trail. Your view is skewed just enough that you see things differently.

Maybe I do know what I'm doing, at least in this one small corner of the world called La Finca Caribe. Yep, it's time I knew that.

Alice's week rolls by with moments of magic sprinkled throughout. Ramses, a friend, stops by with a wooden spatula Jorge has made for Alice, an exact replica of the one she wanted. She is delighted. She is leaving, but she promises to return with her family. They want to take over the whole place with friends and family for a week the next year. She leaves a massive tip earmarked for our giant rubber tree by the gate, establishing what we call the Alice Waters Rubber Tree Maintenance Fund. She blows us kisses and then, like the tiny angel the week before, she's gone.

Years later I still come across her frayed-edge dishcloth serviettes. Guests and other managers are forever mistaking these precious napkins for mere rags. Good lord, no, I explain. They are like holy vestments of a rite of passage for me. I finally get smart and stash them in our private kitchen box for when we come back in the winter. No one seems to treasure them quite like I do.

"Life is very mysterious...and there are many things we don't know. And there are elements of magic realism in every culture, everywhere. It's just accepting that we don't know everything and everything is possible."

—Isabel Allende

Being Here Now, Finally

That winter it feels like I have finally arrived, like I'm walking into the dream I imagined almost twenty years earlier. Although Bill has his own personal connections and deep love of the place, his history with La Finca hasn't been as long or as complicated. He hasn't been thought of as "the crazy lady who bought New Dawn," or "the wild woman who owns La Finca." That's my legacy. With Alice's unknowing help, I begin to own up to what I have built as an innkeeper: the business, my guests, our place in the community, and La Finca itself. I own my ownership differently, and better.

Every so often that winter Bill and I take a night off and go out to dinner or visit friends, maybe go to a party. One evening there is a concert that lots of island folks or, frankly, the North American seasonal snowbirds (like us, but usually more retired) are excited about. It's going to be held in a gallery a ways out of town.

In our early days this building had been home to a great funky bar with awesome local music for dancing. My version of the good old days of Vieques, I guess. But they were good, those days when the island's casual style captured my heart. Back then the open-air dance floor was just a concrete slab with an enormous canopy swaying above, made entirely of beer cans strung together. Christo and Andy Goldsworthy, move over. This moving roof stretched over the whole space, a soft clinking patchwork billowing in the breezes, in sync with the dancers it sheltered below. That was us. People. Locals. Puerto Ricans mostly, and a few expats—those of us who took the time to find the out-of-the-way places. It was all about the music, dancing, and being with your neighbors.

The concert in the art gallery is very different, and so is everything else. The bend in the road used to have a few beat-up cars parked on the shoulder. That's how you knew where the place was. Tonight there is a field filled with shiny new SUVs. I still can't get over how large the average jeep has become, and I still don't know why, or how, two of them navigate around each other on our back roads. "You can't stop progress," Bill says, as he so often does. A parking attendant points us to a remaining spot. The place is packed.

We squeeze into what is now a real room. There haven't been beer cans billowing overhead for years. It's bigger than I remembered, and it's filled with several hundred people and chairs. Packed tight, dressed to the nines, and hot. They are snowbirds, expats, and visiting vacationers, not a lot of locals, as in Puerto Ricans, Viequense. It makes sense. There's not a lot of dancing, and I'm not sure there will be. It may not be that kind of concert. The visiting group is four or five young women from New England. Apparently the large audience relates to their angst and urban whine; I don't. Besides, there's not enough fresh air for me.

I go out and sit on a few steps where I can see the stars. The deep, soft-black night wraps me like a blanket. I feel better already. The wine helps too. The differential between my connection to the night and my disconnection to what's going on inside is so great it's overwhelming. Bill is still inside, so I have no one to talk to about it but the stars. A car alarm goes off. I think, *Back in the day, we were lucky if our windows worked.* I want to write. My phone is, sadly, the closest thing to a journal I have with me, so I pull it out and start tapping away:

did David and i know then that it was on its way out? in some
ways it feels like maybe we did. It meaning the old Vieques.
could we imagine that when we DancEd to Latin bAND unDER the
canopy of cans?? We took Puerto Rican ness of the bar and
dancing neighbors for granted. did i know it was the end of
an era? :(((((
    the music, dancing, and all of us were happy together no?—
that 15 years later we'd be here, where outdoor tavern and
beer canned dance floor was - now now an uber hipster gallery
for upscale epatz and snowbird. everythign seems sad including the performance awkward. not much to do with VQS> people
inside buying art plates from India. theyre asking $500 for
some plate—.do they even know income of locals? Do they know
locals? have we ruined this island? Whats my role in that? did
previous colonists/Spaniard stop and wonder the same thing?
why do gringos want things here to be like they are back hom???
    what does it mean to be in paradise? ****what does Paradise
 mean????)))))))

Bill finds me outside and sits down next to me.

"Is it okay to pine for the olden days, honey?" I ask him, resting my head on his shoulder. "I really don't pine for my youth. I don't want to be young again, but I'd do anything for things to be the same, to be back in the day. Was it as carefree as I remember it? Or am I just romanticizing it all? I'm sad—and why are there so many folks here, when there were four or five other gringos at the EPA meeting this week about developing what should be our protected land? And not many more than that at the meeting about the crime wave? And why don't this many people come to listen to a Puerto Rican band?"

"I don't know, sweetheart," Bill says gently. "Let's get you home."

On the winding way home Bill dodges the potholes he knows as well as he knows the neighborhood dogs he greets most mornings on his runs. It's dark. Our headlights reveal the gnarled red-barked turpentine trees that guide our way.

"You know what I just realized?" I say. "We. Like, you and me, we are colonialists. How dumb are we not to have known that? Does everyone in that room already know that? Or are we colonists?"

I'm trying to compare the two words in my head as I doze off. The next day, I decide to look it up. I need to know more. I need to get a grip on this, at least begin to think about how I fit in with my community: colonist: a settler in or inhabitant of a colony.

Yep—that is most clearly us. All of us who have moved to and inhabited this piece of paradise. Before us, it was the Spanish, the Danes, and the French too. They were perhaps clearer and called it what it was: a colony. The United States apparently doesn't like to use that term (remember, we started off as thirteen colonies ourselves, then kicked our overlords out), so Puerto Rico isn't called a colony. The US government calls it a territory. The Virgin Islands are a US protectorate. The differences are so minimal that Bill and I are left scratching our heads. We have American friends living in Puerto Rico who call themselves ex-pats, but in Puerto Rico we still live under the American flag and have US zip codes.

One hot afternoon Bill and I are on the big house deck when one of the large green jungle iguanas comes scurrying out of the brush. Without moving or saying anything, we watch as he makes his way from bush to agave plant to the solar array, where he hides in the shade of the panels. It's sort of a treat—our kind of home entertainment. The large electric-green iguanas are grotesque and beautiful, depending on your slant on things. They're generally too ornate, too fast, and too much like dinosaurs to be believable, and yet here they are. They aren't native to the island. Originally brought as pets, they escaped. I think back to the morning the boys discovered that our pet iguana, Lisa Simpson, was gone. (Five-year-old Xing Ji bravely fessed up to having left the lid off the cage.) This is likely a relative.

"They act like they own the place," Bill says. He has to clean up after them in the pool several times a week, as they love to go down there to drink, hopefully not to swim.

"And I guess they do. They don't have any natural predators. I don't really like them, but at the same time, I have to confess, I sort of love them."

"I know exactly what you mean," I say. The small dragon continues to patrol his territory. "Like them or not, there's no way we're getting rid of them. They're like us. Oh, my God, Bill!" I've had another epiphany. "We're the iguanas! We are the fantastic, grotesque, invasive species populating with wild abandon, taking over this poor little island with the same confident nonchalance."

In certain respects it doesn't change much to realize one is a colonizer. Maybe everyone is. It's not like I'm going to sell the place or give it back. And back to whom? To the descendants of the colonists who took it from the Taíno people five hundred years ago? They are long gone.

I don't know exactly what to do, but the awareness does make me feel different. From the beginning I felt like a guest on the island. Maybe anyone moving to a different culture does. I tried to be respectful in that I knew I needed to bend to new and different ways rather than expecting them to bend for me. I could never condone the attitude of many fellow Americans who complain when things aren't in English or done the way they are back home. I laugh at folks who think of themselves as true Americans, when it would seem that anyone from this hemisphere, from South, Central, North, or Latin America, can call themselves the same. With this new iguana-like colonial concept, it feels like time to step up to the plate and put a part of my original vision into play.

When I bought La Finca, the island's community needs seemed just as dire and clear as they do today. There's woefully little educational or professional opportunity. I've always felt that Puerto Rico was a good illustration of where the United States is headed, with its focus on shrinking taxes; minimizing education, health care, infrastructure, and natural open spaces; and maximizing corporate ownership and corruption. The schools are drastically underfunded and understaffed.

Years earlier, when we were considering whether to move down, local friends with kids warned me just how lacking the schools were—so bad that when a teacher is sick and misses class, no substitutes are called in, sometimes for weeks on end. Teenage pregnancy, often at age fifteen, is common. Drug use and sales, and the associated crime and violence, are standard practice for the boys. It's what they know. In 1996, in the months before the purchase went through, I vowed to the heavenly powers that if I was lucky enough to get the place, and if it ever made any money, I'd share it with the community. I'd give back as much as could. I envisioned summer camps and weekend workshops, a place where high school students, really kids of all ages, could spend time with role models from all types of professions, from the island, from Puerto Rico, wherever, a place where everything from women's history to environmental best practices, from art and literature to health and nutrition, could be discussed.

Over the years La Finca has given discounts and/or free stays to Puerto Rican school groups whenever we could. Now it's time to turn up the volume, to fulfill my original plan.

With my new self-consciousness as a colonist, an invasive species, it's clear that at the very least we have to better understand, lighten, or improve our impact on this island.

Bill and I start making community meetings and functions a higher priority. We're only there a third of the year, so it's hard to get as involved as we want, but it's a start. It's interesting to see how a career spent doing public awareness in the States translates, or doesn't, to communicating with the Viequense, and where my graduate work in sustainable business practices might apply. It's all worth trying though, and we do. Sometimes our ideas are shot down or ignored for coming from know-it-all gringos. It's understandable. And sometimes our experience is appreciated. We do what we can. Step by slow, iguana-like step.

We go to an annual fundraising dinner to honor the island's most active community leaders. Most of the evening is focused on animal organizations and the good people who work with Vieques's terrible dog and cat problem. We are on board with this, naturally. Then a small, unassuming woman who runs an after-school program for teens, Alcanzando El Éxito (Reach for Success), is introduced. Immediately, my curiosity is piqued. For reasons I can't understand, on Vieques we tend to hear more about the island's needy animals than we do its needy people. The woman, Carmen, is about my age. She grew up on the island but somehow found her way to college in New York. She has spent her career in two worlds—here, and like me, the Pacific Northwest. She introduces a teenage girl who confidently takes the mike and tells her story, in English, to the two hundred people in the room. She talks about how this group has changed her life, how she's going to college now, something no one in her family has ever done.

I start to cry. These are the people in need, and the people doing the work to help them. I go up to them later, introduce myself, and offer La Finca in whatever capacity it can help. Let's get these kids up there for sustainability camps, for role model workshops, whatever. As much as I love dogs, these kids are our future. Hard to imagine a future without them.

I call Carmen the next day, and she invites us to their donated space in Isabel, where they gather after school. The next time I'm in town I stop by and walk in on a meeting the kids are conducting, following strict Robert's Rules. It's a wonderful combination of by-the-book order and laughter. The kids are so different from high schoolers at home. They are exposed to so much less that they actually seem interested in talking with an old lady like me.

We invite them to La Finca to learn about upcycling and simplifying, about alternative careers and ways of running a business. A few of the kids spy Bill's guitar in the corner of our office. Many of them have never held a guitar (or been to a restaurant with menus, or even left the island). The median Viequense family income is less than one-third of that for US families; 35 percent of the people here live in poverty. Many kids come from families with drug and alcohol abuse and untreated mental illness. Others come from steady, working families. Almost across the board, their enthusiasm, manners, and gratitude just to listen to us talk about things we take for granted—like our career or other lifestyle choices—is amazing. They seem interested in everything.

Before long I have started a weekly after-school Green Team with six kids. They are more than familiar with recycling, composting, and the island's solid waste issues. They want to take on building public awareness around the issues and programs on the community radio station.

Meanwhile Bill, with a couple of guitar-playing friends, has formed a group of teens interested in learning to play. We are connecting with people who are not just dedicated to but actively working for change. These are my new role models. I restart my on-and-off Spanish lessons. I am determined to learn more, and to use what I know. The sense of reward from the deeper involvement is incredible, for me and for Bill too—like getting my fingers deep into the soil when I garden. As long as La Finca runs even half this smoothly, we can do this.

It feels like I'm getting close to living in the moment. I am finding my stride, and along with it a new focus. Just when I think I'm getting it, I see how much more there is to learn. And maybe that's a good thing. The day we stop learning—about the property, the island's culture, its ecology and how to leave the softest footprint on it, how to give our guests the best experience, our role and responsibility as citizens in this unique little world—that's when we hand the baton to the kids. Making the beds and cleaning the toilets isn't worth it without the reward of learning.

The finca continues to run smoothly. Knock on wood, praise the Lord or whoever's in charge. We have a great team at the helm for the rest of the year, when we aren't here. Before them, another equally great, experienced, smart, resourceful couple, and the same before them. With any luck it will continue. We've turned our big corner, it seems. We have slowly found our way to number 1 on our specialty lodging category on TripAdvisor. Each new managing couple garners the same enthusiastic, stellar reviews. Each entry describes them as "absolutely the best." And that's good. We like when our managers and guests are happy. Managers last longer now. They stay on in our lives as friends. They come back as guests or vacation relief. They are retired or semiretired folks, or people wanting to learn how to shed their careers. With any luck, La Finca teaches them a thing or two, like it does us.

There are the ongoing lessons in how to live quietly, just the two of us, entertaining ourselves without the hustle and bustle of life back home. Learning the joys of living in a two-room indoor/outdoor cabin with simple meals, simple days for months at a time, is a good thing for me. Bill's drawing table is a piece of plywood balanced on milk crates on the bed. A large, plastic storage bin serves as a dresser. I never cared too much about

fashion—makeup and jewelry—but living without even thinking of any of it is liberating. I'm not sure I should mention shedding bras and shaving—some things are so controversial!—but my guardian angel doesn't wear a bra, that's for sure. And I'm not sure she shaves.

It's weird...I'm in love with a piece of land.

Oh how I love thee, Finca

I shall count a dozen ways...

The way you play hide and seek with St. Croix.
Now you see it, now you don't.

The way you gave
my kids their own wild
place in the world.

The way you keep secrets, like
the quiet beauty of dawn; how
it unfolds — pale apricot
across your deck.

The way you teach me like a gentle,
patient grandmother would, turning
me to the lesson, until I get it right.

The way you introduced me to Latin
America, and her daughter Puerto Rico.

I love your graciousness,
the way you serve it up and
make the local beer and coffee taste great.

That you seem as comfortable being
quiet for writing, yoga, and meditation, as
you do whooping it up in laughter or dance.

That your natural
beauty helps the rest of us feel
comfortable without the makeup
and whatnot from home.

And that you only get more beautiful the older you get.

21.

The Winter Things Couldn't Get Right

Things don't always go smoothly. Sometimes dog paddling is necessary, and sometimes a dead man's float will do it. Whatever it takes to stay up and hopefully get to the other side. Today it's a hard long crawl.

It's the first three weeks of December, usually slow and sort of sweet in their predictability. It's not a dead calm, but it's leisurely, with just one or two guests for a few days. Fair sailing for travelers and innkeepers alike, calm seas and wide vistas. I'm always telling friends that December, before the holidays, is a great time to travel. Not too many take advantage of it. Guess that's why it stays great. Empty. Cheap. But we take advantage of it.

Most years Bill and I arrive on December 1, catch our breath, shake off the chill from home, and get to work. We have nearly three weeks to batten down any hatches and finish whatever the managers started in the fall. We overlap with them for a week or two, and then they take off to pursue their adventures. We have time to see our island friends and get to the beach before the storm of Christmas guests blows in, followed by New Year's, and then on and on, like swells. As foreseeable as any other in the Caribbean, high season lasts until Easter. Our guests rain down in torrents. In squalls. Sometimes slowing to just a steady drizzle. In patterns, like the families that storm though in mid-February and March for winter and spring breaks. But like everywhere else, climate change is causing this pattern to shift.

This year things don't go according to plan. The largest group we've ever hosted, for the longest time—thirty-eight international sustainable-business students staying for ten days—checks in the day after we arrive. There's no time for us to discover that the trees and shrubs are covering the solar panels for the shower system (no hot water for twenty of the guests bunking in the main house) or the infestation of ticks in one cabin (courtesy of a dog we'd naively agreed to keep months earlier). They'd actually been discovered and eradicated—*completo!*—in the summer, or so we were told. "All natural. All effective. Totally guaranteed." All good—as in not. Not gone. Not good. And not like *anything* had ever dealt with.

"*No te preocupes*," Felix, the third exterminator we are trying, tells me. "Don't worry. It's been a really bad year for them. Most hotels have had them." He smiles and adds, "Even the fancy ones."

This makes me feel better, a little less than suicidally embarrassed, for a whole thirty seconds. Then I go back to trying to remain calm and drum up a solution. The place is booked to the hilt. There is no other house, cabin, room, or cot where we can put the five gals (in fact, the retreat's staff). We find a house to rent in town at our expense, $1,000 a week—call it our profit margin—but the group leader, Suki, understandably doesn't want to leave the group.

We are in our office trying to deal with the situation discreetly, for all our sakes. We've been discreet in our schlepping all suitcases and all contents in tightly tied garbage bags across the property, to the laundry for washing. Discreet in not letting anyone come close to the building, discreet in ushering the fumigation trucks through the gate to the far corner of the property.

There's only one bunk vacant—our futon couch. The one in our office, which is really our living room and the other half of our kitchen, depending on which side of the bamboo screen you're on, and two feet from our cabin's bathroom. We've only got a pull-out couch for those crazy times when our kids visit and we're booked for a day or two of their stay. It's for family emergencies. Oh, God—this may qualify.

Suki comes over and sees the futon. Within the hour she moves into our cabin. Hard to know whether she is grateful for the bed or just hates us.

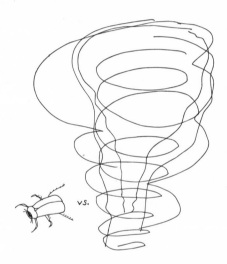

"june bug vs. hurricane"

It's awful. None of us have an ounce of privacy or escape for ten long days. The only thing that saves us is that the students are fellows from as far away as Nepal, Bali, Switzerland, and Ecuador or as close as Haiti, who were given this free week to brainstorm in the Caribbean. They are going to be so easy and fun. And they are. It isn't their fault everything that can go wrong does.

I sit out here and write for an hour next to one guy, a guest I've barely spoken to, every morning. Neither of us says a word after "good morning." We write and let the morning unveil what it will. The mysterious unknown birds chirp and screech, calling all around us. Sometimes we hear just the flapping of their wings, or the roosters, and the faintest of songs from a boom box at the farm across the way.

There's a lingering smell of beer from whatever guests were doing until the wee hours last night. The place looks to be in shambles, but it's only superficial stuff. The deck and rails are strewn with wet, sandy beach towels, dirty dishcloths, journals, coffee cups, water bottles, various devices and phones, cameras, and large-format paper easels for brainstorming. Think organic frat house. I can rise above my inclination to mom it.

To sit quietly is a joy, especially after the noise that comes from such a large group. The music, the chatter. My outside desk is so near the deck where they've been giving their workshops that I've been an unknown participant. I've sat through their quiet meditations, their mission statement writing, pitch-making, and personality tests. Without trying, I'm hidden by the plants and the sheet of plywood they've been using as their white board. Think Post-its, hundreds and hundreds of them. Some still sticking to org charts and paradigms, others blowing around the property. Neon pink squares snuggled into the bromeliads. And Sharpies and other tools to facilitate their brainstorming. Think Pandora streaming all day. Think eye masks and earplugs. All odd tools for being at this place.

Funny thing is, though, they're a great group. Just the kind of group I envisioned hosting, way back when—folks coming here to think up ways to save the world.

This quiet time is precious. Soon folks will wake up, and duty calls. Time now for fresh dishcloths, recycling, and compost bins. But sounds like already they're stumbling out, looking for coffee. I thought after whooping it up until 2 a.m. they'd be starting late this morning. No such luck. My quiet time will have to wait until tomorrow.

We push through—like a long, hard labor. The week is finally over, and despite it all most of the guests are still smiling when they leave. Bill and I are utterly exhausted. What should have

PRAYER FOR A REALLY BAD DAY

Please, Powers that Be, I rarely ask for anything, but I'm begging you. **HOW ABOUT** today things go differently? How about — if there isn't a guest sleeping on our couch? The couch being right next to the bathroom door, so that we have to walk next to her the two or three times we use the bathroom each night. How about she's not the lead contact from the most prestigious university we've hosted, here for an international symposium on sustainability? How about there isn't an outbreak of ticks, our first ever! — for God's sake — in her and her staff's cabin? How about she takes advantage of the apartment we rented for them in town. **HOW ABOUT** the funny feeling in my mouth from all the chemicals I sprayed goes away? — I find time to brush my teeth? — the pest control guy tells me he was kidding about having to burn the cabin down to get rid of these bugs? That'd be good. **HOW ABOUT** today the shrubs don't block the solar panels — so the 15 people in the main house can take a warm shower? Or, we go back in time and figure this out before they get here, like the tree guy might get here earlier than the day before they leave? How about today our wifi works? Maybe it will now that we figured it's the volume of continual demand on it, like their constant backdrop of playlists drowning out the crickets and frogs. HOW ABOUT the Internet guy, the gardener, and the exterminator answer their phones? How about the two uber-urban guys staying in the casita don't continue to notice a funny smell coming from their sink drain? ... The one where I couldn't smell a thing but doused it all in vinegar and baking powder, smiling, all eco-friendly and confident this would do the job, regardless of the fact that I couldn't figure out what the job was that needed doing... **HOW ABOUT** Bill and his crew won't decide to set up their band saw on the front porch of Casa Nueva at 8 a.m., so the gals staying up there have one more totally legitimate thing to complain about and don't have to walk through the ripping buzzing noise and sawdust when they go in and out of their place? **HOW ABOUT** this sickly, half-starved feral kitty doesn't keep begging at the back door? HOW ABOUT my attitude changes and I find energy to answer guest calls? Maybe I don't go ahead with the plan of blocking out the remaining open days on the calendar to prevent others from coming for the rest of this month. **HOW ABOUT** if the annual African bee swarm doesn't start up outside, or is it inside, my shower wall? 'Cause something in there is starting to buzz. How about just maybe, there won't be bugs flitting in and around my bed when I'm ready to read tonight? Maybe I could find an app that turns off the bug appeal of the screen glow. And maybe I'll find time to write...

been the coolest week ever was truly the most trying. The ticks seem to be gone. But still we've had to move or cancel weeks of incoming guests. And the fun doesn't stop.

The moment we are ushering—more like pushing—the last of the students out the gate, the Victoria's Secret film crew arrives for their annual catalog shoot, as well as some broadcast special they will shoot here. Yes, you read that right. And you don't keep crew or talent waiting. Not these glamorous boys and girls. They are important. We are not. They are called Angels. Some of them are famous. They make millions a year.

The recalled memories of the tension and hype around this film shoot generates posttraumatic stress for me. The egos in film and video are virtually unparalleled in any industry except fashion, and for this shoot we have both, with an extra layer of sexist exploitation.

The crew wants the van to drive up to the house. We don't usually let vehicles drive on the grass, but they have lots of equipment they don't want to haul across the lawn.

"No problem!" I say, trying to sound upbeat and welcoming. Bedraggled or not, I am their hostess.

"Thanks," the production assistant from London says. He sounds grateful. "The Angels don't like to walk that far."

Huh? We are talking about fifty yards. I don't say a word. They are paying us well. It'll be fine.

The shoot goes about as well as it could. Bill is in bed with the flu most of the time, so I am on hand to help with whatever. These kinds of Angels don't smile or talk or look you in eye, but one does ask me for water. I've thought ahead and have a large pitcher of ice water with lemon.

"You bet," I say, and point to it, with stacks of glasses on a brightly enameled Mexican tray. They are here for our funky hipness, after all. I've learned to make it look pretty, and I always add lemon.

"I meant bottled," she says.

"Nope, sorry," I say. That's a lie. I'm not sorry. I don't believe in plastic bottles.

Luckily the Angels don't stay at La Finca, nor do their crews. Along with the creative crew from London, the Florida crew, and the technical crew from San Juan, they stay at the island's faux luxury corporate hotel. They are shooting at spots around the island as well as here.

They make smoothies at a juice bar they rig up on our deck for the "vibe" of the place. La Finca is a backdrop. It's for their TV special or maybe their catalog. I can't keep it straight. I just know that La Finca looks like what they want the Caribbean to look like. It's fine if they don't stay here. It means fewer beds to make. And we are exhausted, like never before. Knowing our tolerance for work and what we've pushed ourselves through, that's saying a lot.

Later that week, however . . .

"Bill? Bill?" Someone in my dream is exceedingly inappropriate. I'm jealous. Why is she asking for my man? "Bill!" It's a whisper, somehow urgent.

My thick wall of consciousness is finally cracked with a knock on the door. Bill doesn't wake up. It's Susan, one of the guests. It's 4 a.m. This means trouble. Or, as Susan explains, yelling from our front porch, "The smoke alarm in our cabin is beeping. It's too high for me to reach."

By now she could be waking up the whole main house right next door. I rouse Bill, who gets dressed enough to walk back with her. Luckily, Susan is a regular, a wonderful winter fixture. She and her ninety-three-year-old boyfriend come for a month every January. And our main house guests are all really cool right now. To make myself stay awake until Bill gets back (something to do with being a supportive wife, or looking like one), I do an inventory of our current guests:

Room 1: Totally fun hipster tech blogger and toy designer from Austin, partiers. Recovering Mormons. They'll go with the flow.

Room 2: General store owner in rural Wisconsin. Nice gal, my age. This may be her third stay with us. She's cool, sort of becoming part of the family.

Room 3: Two young Canadian women; very urban, serious fashionistas. They keep to themselves so I don't know what they do professionally or much else. They frequent the fancier places every night. Didn't appreciate our advice about not wearing long flowing skirts and platform sandals for kayaking on the bio-bay. They might mind the noise, but they are on the farthest corner. I think we're safe. (Note: They will go on to write our worst review in years and years. They said I didn't clean the bathrooms. I think it was payback for me asking them to keep their toiletries in the rooms, not the bathroom. Luckily it was in French—*mais mon Dieu!* A single star hurts our five-star average!)

Room 4: Sweet couple, two guys from Philly. Florist and nurse. High on the self-sufficient fun meter. Also repeat guests. Casual, easygoing.

Room 5: Empty.

Room 6: Sylvia, our dear friend and restaurant designer from San Juan, and her boyfriend, an amazing modern oil painter. Awesome. Couldn't be happier and more interesting.

But, then, "couldn't be happier and more interesting" goes for most of them. They either arrive that way or get that way after a day or two, including Susan and Ed. They are pretty darn sweet about this craziness. None of the others will notice or mind the middle-of-the-night disturbance.

As tough as it gets, I love how direct and immediate our work is. I can't figure out if it's hedonistic or Buddhist, but it's all about sharing joy. People come here to have fun, to relax, to share special time with families, friends, themselves. Our job is to share a space that helps them do that. Hopefully that's without a freak bug invasion, and with the lights and smoke alarms all working. Should be pretty darn simple.

A few folks arrive really out of sorts. Traveling can be hard, especially after a couple of flights or time zones. But it only takes a day for the tension to fall away. With certain guests, Bill and I sometimes take on a challenge and bet each other a beer if we can get the gal in the cabanita to smile. One of us usually can.

Charlie's view from New Dawn. 2/9?
J. Turner

Some of those are the ones who have changed my life, and certainly my way of think-ing about things: Guests keep you honest. With the internet, the almost constant threat of a bad review looms large. It keeps you on your toes. But you also have to be honest with yourself. It's not just learning to give but also to receive, even complaints, gra-ciously. And also how to say no, I can't drive you to the airport on Christmas morning.

Bill is back. We can go back to sleep.

It happens again two nights later, at 1 a.m. Same gal. Both times she's had to walk across the property to tell us. Poor thing. Who put a second smoke alarm in the caban-ita? Why, God, why? Why any of it?

Nothing else goes wrong. Probably because nothing else can; we have fixed every-thing and it's only December. And out of the heavenly blue, we have the day off. Finally, a moment to breathe! The three-day photo shoot turned into two; the producers don't like the day's lighting. So today is truly a paid holiday, sandwiched like heaven between two insane circuses. Bill and I escape for dinner to one of our favorite restaurants in Isabel. Conuco is owned and run by a family from San Juan. It's the kind of place where they remember your name and greet you with hugs. The food is great, and there isn't an ounce of attitude. Nothing is precious, just good. Bill always admires details in the building and its renovation. It turns out that the father of the great chef is an architect and teaches at the University of Puerto Rico. Figures. He kept the original old colonial house's exterior but opened it up inside to be more like a modern version of a classic, simple country house. Como una finca. No wonder we love it.

The interior is like a newer, cleaner version of our place. Corrugated metal roofing over simple frame construction, open-air windows with heavy, natural wood shutters, tall doors, high ceilings. "I still wish we'd gotten these fans for Casa Nueva," Bill says, settling into his dark rum and tonic. I'm halfway through my tequila with lime.

"The ugly ones Tito put in will break before long, hon." I say. "Besides, when you think about the other things that went wrong with that building, the fans are hardly our biggest problem."

We laugh. We always do. Casa Nueva was supposed to be so cool. Funny to think that we had been dating less than a year when we embarked on the idea of building it. "The best part is that we were naive enough to think we'd retire to just live in that building. Remember?"

"Yep. And not work. We were supposed to just live in that building and not work. Ha!"

"We thought we'd get away with being the gracious hosts, the somewhat retired inn-keepers up the hill. We'd come down to say hi and have a drink with the guests—when we were back from the beach." We clink our glasses again on that one.

"We were supposed to write, draw, and play the guitar. I love that dream!" Bill says.

And then we both get it. Both of us sit there, looking at each other. Neither of us notices when the ceviche arrives. Vanessa, our waitress, is asking if we'd like to order, but we just look at each other, realizing it's time.

"Maybe the next lesson is letting go? And doing less, not more?" I venture.

How funny to think about that—we're always so proud of how hard we work, and how hands-on we are. How we send our managers off while we step in to do everything ourselves. What if it just means we are totally neurotic? When unknowing friends refer to us as being on vacation, our favorite comeback is to clarify that it's no vacation, and no picnic—we're a staff of two. I clean the toilets, Bill fixes them. It's like we need to make sure they know how proletarian we are. We may be semiretired snowbirds, but we are hardworking, maniacal snowbirds. Are we addicted to the work? Do we even know how to relax?

"I wonder if we could be just as proud of not working so hard," Bill says. "How do we fill our time? Or is that just way too hedonistic?"

"I don't know. Let's find out."

We finally order and go on to strategize throughout the meal and ride home how we can retire from this working retirement. The dream, the plan I hatched way back when, turning forty, driving in the Saab over the Cascades, was all about being the innkeeper. But that was before I met La Finca, before I walked through the gate.

Here I am turning sixty, driving over different hills with a different husband in a different life—sort of. I don't feel old. I'm not exactly falling apart, but not young. It's the third chapter, time to let myself off the hook; let others explain that Chivas and Blue

Beach are the same thing, point the direction, and recommend a place where they can go for lunch along the way.

"How about next winter, the managers stay on?" I say. "They stay in the manager's cabin and continue to run the place. And we just live at La Finca. It'll cost us—our salary, and the rent from whichever of the houses we're in. And if it's Casa Nueva, that means our best house." I'm not backing out; I just want to make sure we can pull this off.

"Who cares?" Bill says, "We can finally funkify it—Finca-fy it. We can do all the things we ever wanted to do to it, or not. You may just want to go to paddleboarding or write."

Just when I'm afraid the meatiest lessons are behind us, I figure it out. This letting go, doing less, might be the most interesting one yet.

HOW DID I DO IT?
MINE WAS A 20-STEP & 20-YEAR PROGRAM:

Work hard

Ask a lot of your kids

Forgive a lot

Ask to be forgiven more

Ignore the naysayers

Don't stop your Spanish lessons

Don't borrow money from the Tong

Find a great therapist

Share roast chicken on Sundays

Hire smart people

Keep a journal

Throw the I Ching

Take checks

Watch the sunrise as often as you can

Trust the people you trust

Don't trust the people you don't

Trust your nose

Go for the guy who isn't your type

When all else fails — find, create, and share joy

Do it all until humble is your middle name.

Then repeat, until it's your first

22.

How & ¿Por Qué?

It would be impossible to count how many times I've been asked how and why I did this. It's taken more than two decades to answer. So for those inquiring minds who ask, mine was a twenty-step program.

A lot can happen to a gal in twenty years—or to a family, or a small Caribbean island. When we got to Vieques in 1996, it wasn't included on most maps of the Caribbean. I called it "almost undiscovered," and all of us were young in our different ways. You could wear cutoffs and flip-flops anywhere on the island, and no one thought you were authentic or on-trend for doing so. There were no shopping opportunities; restaurants were open-air shacks, mostly. The beaches were empty and wild. And La Finca was part of all that.

Now I refer to the island as "changing" and La Finca as "rustic," to help distinguish it from what newcomers are calling "luxury." What a funny term. One man's shadow is another's shade, and all that. I hear folks asking where to get dry cleaning done, or whether you need to fumigate your house if you see a scorpion. Infinity pools, security surveillance systems, and dressing up for expensive restaurants never meant luxury to me. It all sounds like imprisonment.

I feel at my most luxurious when I can grab an evening swim alone in the pool. Granted, our pool is cracked and discolored, with a few missing tiles. But if you look up as you float on your back, you can ignore all that. You can forget the pool installer who never came back to finish the job, the repairers since who ripped you off, the caretakers who tried to hide the dog hair in the filter, or the parties where guests smoked so much dope on the pool house roof that they dove from it into the six-foot "deep" end. Shudder. Or the frat house group who put the garden furniture in the pool one night. Or the reality show crew who doused their teen stars in olive oil before rolling them down the grass hill and into the pool, assuring that the resulting matted green globs went into the water and ultimately into the pump.

This pool, this place, has been through a lot. Kind of like all of us. But if I let myself look up long enough I can forget that—and the new designer vacationers running all over the island searching for an "authentic but air-conditioned" restaurant. When I do forget, and I'm blessed with a jet-black, star-studded sky, I find my full-on, dream-come-true luxury setting. I'm living larger, luckier, than I ever dared to imagine. Dreams can come true when you work really hard and then let go. And I am grateful to my warm, floating bones.

I look at Vieques, at La Finca, our guests, at Bill and our kids, and I look in the mirror. All of us growing, aging, and changing over the years, trying to stay true to our course amid the craziness, learning to be careful what we wish for. But why? I'm still not sure I understand the reason, the why behind it. I like to think about it, though. I like to think about the choices we make and the choices that make us, the dreams that drive them. I'm intrigued by the signposts we choose to read and the flashing orange warning lights we pretend not to see. And then there are the ones in Spanish that you'd better learn if you want to be here.

I am still driven by some internal force, that's for sure. Is it that my guardian angel or just my strong-willed, rebellious mother's spirit? Or maybe in those first four years together, maybe it was something my cowboy dad said. Maybe before he died he whispered in my ear about the importance of loving a piece of land and learning all you could from it. Maybe a cowboy's daughter is a cowgirl even after he and the cows are gone. Maybe the southern view of that big, blue Caribbean Sea, stretching south from the main deck, maybe that's my open range and this finca my own tropical Red River Valley.

Whether I got it from my mom or my dad, my awesome siblings, or my amazing kids, I learned it, but in my heart. Something made me know that we needed this adventure as much as it needed us, that I needed to learn all that it's taught me and still teaches me. When the learning slows, I look forward to handing this bit of paradise on to the kids, for that whisper of the legacy, that swishing rustle of a palm tree, comes with it.

For La Finca, I have channeled my inner Joan of Arc. For her, for our guests, I have raced across the property to interrupt a domestic issue, forgetting that the loud, angry German boyfriend is more than six feet tall and I am merely me, in my muumuu, before coffee. No matter. I got him off the property. To defend my beautiful finca, I have risen in the darkest of nights and run up to the sound of scary men's voices muttering softly in the jungle, charging without fear right up to them, demanding to know what they were doing hidden behind the cars. Clearly they were bandits about to invade, and I was armed with nothing more than my righteous love of the place. Mother Bear innkeeper.

It turns out, of course, that they were yoga instructors arriving early for the next day's retreat who'd taken a predawn boat and didn't have anywhere else to go.

Okay, so sometimes it does get a little out of hand. The point is, the love is deep. The finca is such a deep part of me that I can't imagine life without it, and I would do anything for it. It, she, that little corner of the world makes all those years of craziness and hardship okay. More than okay.

A river of love runs through the place, and gratitude as well. I never have stopped counting my lucky stars—and there are many to count. I'm the lucky gal who got La Finca and all that comes with it.

Thank you all / Muchas gracias todos

to our guests, managers, children,

island friends, and neighbors;

to all who make up La Finca;

the lizards, birds, pets,

even the tarantulas, and occasional iguanas;

all those who wander through.

GRACIAS

Epilogue

This book took me a lifetime to learn and about six years to write. It sat, pretty much finished, on my desk for just over two years waiting for one of my epiphanies, something to help me write the epilogue. Not all books have to have an epilogue, but this one did. It kept having them. Just when I'm getting close, splash! There I go sliding off that stepping-stone into the water again—where I am pulled along by the current until I find something to hold on to and drag my sorry drenched self out again. Oh! So that's the real ending. That's the lesson learned—the epilogue! When splash!—and again I'm sliding off.

A month after I finished the manuscript—on that lofty happy note, where I'd figured out on the last page that I was the lucky lady who got La Finca—Bill was hospitalized with abdominal pain. Within a few weeks he was diagnosed with pancreatic cancer, the bad kind. The kind where it's a matter of time, and not much time at that. Funny how your life's work can suddenly stop mattering at all. I shoved the manuscripts and journals, collages, postcards, photographs, bits of rice paper, quotes, and kids' art into folders and boxes. My book—and managing La Finca, which usually took precedence in my day—were both suddenly completely irrelevant. I became caretaker to my husband as he fought cancer with chemo and surgeries and everything else we could throw at it. We never ran La Finca again. I think we came through and grabbed some of our things on our way home from the hospital. I don't quite remember.

I am not going to tell that story here. Trying to capture the cocooned tunnel of cancer and caretaking, of dining with death at the table every night is too big. Learning to be unafraid of—and help your partner right up to—the thing we have been afraid of our whole lives, or trying to avoid, in every book, movie, TV show, or nightmare, is a different story. This is the tale of La Finca. Suffice it to say, in the middle of the long, slow, sad process of watching my husband die, I wasn't thinking about La Finca much.

Bill died a year and a half later. With cancer you see death coming and you plan for it. You plan for the grief. I started to grieve at the diagnosis. Even as I tried to live in the moment, a part of every moment seemed to hold the future questions, What about me? What would the rest of my life look like?

Although La Finca took a backseat to these priorities, as Bill's passing got closer I realized that without him, La Finca would be landing on my shoulders—alone again. I'd already learned those lessons. I knew it was too much to handle alone. At the same time, I knew it would be the best place to heal. The place where I could start to transition to my next self. Whoever that would be.

Swinging in Room 3's hammock would have to work its magic again, like it had before, the last time life fell apart, twenty years earlier. I'd make myself sway until I'd seen enough shooting stars to let myself go to bed. Between that nightly ritual and keeping busy with guests, I might even have fun. At least I would somehow get through. Knowing I had that hammock to fall into was invaluable. That was the plan. As if there could be a plan.

Six weeks after Bill died, as I was getting the barn ready to host his memorial, La Finca died, obliterated by Hurricane Maria and her unprecedented two-hundred-mile-an-hour Category 5 strength. Of course, I didn't know that then. All I knew was that a storm the size of Texas had been poised to strike Vieques a week before. We had heard nothing since, but over the years I'd learned to be okay with that.

With Hurricane Irma a few weeks before, we'd lost some trees and roofing. The power was still out when Maria hit. It had been hard to get much phone time with our managers, Bill and Scott, but I knew they were seriously prepared. They were hunkered into Casa Nueva, the one we had designed as our hurricane hole, for this second big storm. Maria was on my mind as I placed the chairs and hay bales in a spiraling circle for folks to sit and celebrate Bill's life in the barn. But I wasn't too worried. Surrounded by every loved one I had, circled up with a heavy fall rain pelting our metal barn, I actually joked about living with the unknown of Maria's damage.

In the days after that, small bits of information started getting through. Random texts from people I didn't know: "Corky, we were finally able to drive by your place. I'm so sorry." Or, "There are pieces of blue lumber a half mile down the road. I think they are part of La Finca." No word from Bill and Scott.

Inexplicably, surreally, NASA aerial photographs came through on the web, showing raw dirt and white pipes where the main house was supposed to be. The image did something to my heart, and something else to my gut. I wailed. The main house was eliminated off the planet. That and the manager's cabin, and even the gate. Remember the portal I'd walked through that changed my life? It wasn't knocked over, it wasn't lying broken on the dirt road. It was just gone. How's that for a poetic epilogue?

Nothing could have braced me for those first satellite pictures. The main house. Big Blue. Casa Grande. The plywood palace. Whatever you had called it, however you had known it, whatever of its rooms or hammocks you'd preferred, whether you liked the big deck out back or the front porch looking through the bananas, whether you'd like to cook on the gas stove with flames that sputtered in the open breezes or preferred the steadiness of the electric, no matter which stove, deck, room, banana plant, or swinging bench you loved—or even a cherished book you'd borrowed from its lending library—it was all gone. The satellite pictures showed a messy smudge of stuff, a debris field spread over the half the property. Pretty much garbage and memories were the only things left. I could sort of make out the other houses. What should have been roofs on some looked more like floors. It was hard to get a clear picture from space and harder still to get a clear sense from four thousand miles away, alone and grieving in my cabin.

I wail like I've heard tribal women do, keening for loved ones. Bill's death was so slow. I'd been prepared—the tears for Bill had been shed on and off for the past two years. But this loss is a complete shock. I feel like I've lost half my body, like I've been sawn in half. At this age do I still have to pretend to be strong? I have to tell the kids who are scattered across the country. We all lose it. All flights into and out of Puerto Rico have been canceled, but someone finally figures out there is intermittent cell coverage if you can get high enough in the hills. With that, they post a list of people who have been seen and are safe. Bill and Scott's names are among those, thank God.

It starts to soak in, in pieces, I've lost my finca, my other soulmate, my fourth child, my teacher, healer, the main character in my book. I actually remember being distraught about having to rewrite the book. The losses keep popping up. I'd lost my perfect working retirement, my identity, my role in the community, my escape from the Pacific Northwest winter's gloom, my ability to support all those schools and nonprofit groups who stayed with us. Fuck. There was no other word for it, and it didn't come close. It was all gone. Like the gate. Without it, I didn't know where I was or which direction to go.

From my comfortable cabin on the Olympic Peninsula, I try to wrap my head around it. I try to remember. I try to forget. I try to figure out how to get down there, how I'll move forward. Expecting to be my busy innkeeper self over the coming winter is the one thing I've been relying on for this first winter of widowhood. My plan of submerging myself in my old role to ease into the new role of widow is shot.

I've been low before and I've handled loss, lots of loss. I've become downright good at it, or so they tell me. But this a new low. I try to get over the feeling that everything is my fault, or all about me. I figure that even my own weird karma can't have caused a hurricane, so how does that work? A friend on Vieques tells me that she hasn't been looted because she's a good person. What does that say about me?—because as the fall wears on, almost everything at La Finca that wasn't destroyed is looted. Every solar panel, every power tool, the washing machine; even our antique red bench is discovered at a beachfront bar in town.

I think about my role, about karma. I am the risk-taker, the crazy lady who owned an uninsurable wooden house in the Caribbean. The one without doors or locks. It was a great goddamn ride while it lasted. Better to have lived without locks and lose it all

than never have . . . You know the rest. You can't complain about getting burned if you play with matches, eh? I own my part in all of it.

But I get stuck on wondering about all that finca magic. Where did it go? What is the legacy from here? The thing I can't seem to answer, or begin to understand, is, where is the kitchen? And if there is no kitchen, where is the frying pan, the huge cast-iron one? This becomes my Zen koan. Where are the handmade wooden drawers marked "forks" and "knives" and "etc." from the kitchen? If you've ever stayed or cooked in the main house, you know what I mean. I keep thinking about the space—the air—that once held the kitchen. That amazing kitchen with the hammock right outside the window. I think of the deck, and playing charades, all the dancing that took place there. How on earth can that be over, how can it not exist anymore? The next time I hear the Buena Vista Social Club, I start to wail again, from that bottomless pit of loss.

A month later travel restrictions to Puerto Rico open up, but flights into and out of Vieques are limited. The airport is too hurt; the ferries are too damaged. On Vieques the roads are closed, and so is the hospital. Emergencies are being handled in a tent. People have died from lack of medical attention. Everyone on the island is without power, fresh food or water, phones, or gas for transportation and generators. FEMA and the National Guard arrive with packages of emergency K-rations they toss from the road. Neighbors don't know how neighbors are doing. Family members who live in different parts of the island are unable to communicate. The only way to glean basic information is to check a few local bulletin boards. I wait.

When more flights start again, authorities and friends agree that it is still unwise to go. There is still no fresh water. Cholera has been reported on the main island. It's not safe, and without building supplies or tools I wouldn't be able to make repairs. I've learned that our cars are trashed, so we would have no mode of transportation even if there were gas.

By winter the boys and I are finally able to fly to Puerto Rico. Gus goes down like a commando to scope out the situation. If nothing else, he needs to meet the small group of Rastas who have moved onto the property. Scott and Bill have finally given up trying to live at the finca and have moved to town, where they can at least get rations and information. Before they left, they asked a few dreadlocked guys they met on the beach if they'd prefer broken-down shacks in the hills to hammocks on the beach. At this point even I can see the dark humor in this. I've had every other sort of caretaker, so why not a bunch of Rasta beach bums I've never met?

Gus comes back, chanting Bob Marley's "One Love," totally amazed by the volunteer effort the Rastas have put into the place. Delivering a six-page almost scientific analysis of the situation, he gives us the go-ahead for initial work parties. Okay. I am determined to rebuild whatever we can, and the kids are determined to help.

"We got this, Mom." Xing Ji, now with a preschooler and new baby of her own, cannot go down but cheerleads our efforts from afar. "We will save the finca, Mom. We will make all pretty." Xing smiles at this line, which she'd said a hundred times before, starting at five years old, when the two of us would make the beds and clean the rooms. She'd always add a little bunch of fresh flowers in a jar for incoming guests. "Make all pretty, Mommy."

Driving up, I see what looks to be a house next to the banana grove, but it is upside down. And crushed. Our old electric oven is in the middle of the parking area, sitting where Maria had tossed it five months earlier. Walking onto the property, from where the gate used to be, I see the rubble. Above it, empty air that once was the kitchen, the wraparound deck, Room 3. All the rooms. If you look uphill, it's all air; if you look downhill, a debris field.

My compass rose–painted floor from the main lobby is skewered on a tree near the bottle wall, up by the front gate. Does it point a way out and through all this? I wonder. Nothing seems real. The swinging benches are crushed. Everything is crushed and beginning to rot. The book library, the front desk, the brochures, the bins full of T-shirts for sale are wet and moldy or dried out and bleached, depending on their position in the strata of junk. Days later, rifling through, I find the frying pan—rusty as hell, but not looted, so maybe I'm not a bad person. We find the wooden silverware drawers. A small strip of duct tape at the back and they'll be fine, I think.

In coming weeks and months, past guests and friends circle around me and the kids and the finca, offering more love and support than I could have ever imagined. People want to help. I begin to see the magic glimmering. Complete strangers share their love, money, and time. We organize work parties, inviting friends, family, guests, and any other willing characters to work their asses off and call it fun. Our goal is to get the one standing house, Casa Nueva, organized so volunteer friends and past guests can stay to repair, rebuild, and clean. This also includes clearing the land, hauling away debris that must be dismantled with power tools—debris that fills sixty truckloads destined for the dump.

We buy a truck for the hauling, and in some ways that becomes the last straw. I'm driving home from town with Gus when the brakes go out. That's when I have that feeling in my gut, and I know the party is finally over. Or it will be if we make it back alive.

Even with all three kids almost desperately committed to salvaging the place, it just might not be feasible. Puerto Rico had been devastated. Our Isla Nena had been hit hard, and La Finca was one of the worst and most-devastated sites. Without knowing it, I'd prophesied accurately when I wrote in a blog that "love was easier to find than building materials on Puerto Rico." Eight months after the hurricane, we'd flown down to reroof and discovered there were still no roofing materials available. Whatever tool we reached for, whatever material or process we needed, it wasn't available. Breathe deep. *Poco a poco.* Were we in fact moving forward, making any progress at all?

But when those goddamn brakes went out, I'd had it. Keep in mind that this was the good truck. Not like all the other so-called good trucks we'd bought over the years. This was a really, really good truck we'd bought from the really good guy, the really, really good friend we could really trust. I looked over at Gus, in between the white-knuckled downhill curves, scared as all get-out. "Honey," I said, "even La Finca may not be worth dying for."

We did the odd math with Ty and Xing on the phone that night. We tallied our emotions, logistics, and finances. Without the main house there was no real way to make it work. Not unless we lived there and worked at it full time. My children were each forging their new careers, and I was so tired. The weight of it all, the debris, the loss, it seemed completely beyond me. I had no idea of the solution or how I could maintain long enough to find one.

But as we'd seen so many times before, La Finca magic is real, like the time the groceries showed up for Alice Waters's visit. I didn't make that up. Remember Sylvia? The guest who loved the place so much she opened an inn inspired by it in San Juan? The one who sent over lamps and bedspreads from her movie shoots to spiff up the place? The one who had readied the place for the large group when the managers went missing on a kayak trip? Sylvia, my friend from San Juan, arrived with a volunteer crew from her place. With her resources, brains, and energy, she'd figure out what we could do.

Or maybe I figured it out myself.

I ran to hug Sylvia as she walked from the car. It was her first time seeing the place destroyed. It could be overwhelming, and I held her long and hard. Sylvia had always coveted La Finca. She had always called Casa Nueva her house.

"Sylvia, do you still want the place?" I whispered to her through the long sad hug.

"*Claro que sí, chica.* Of course I do."

And with that I let go. The finca's future would be in her hands now.

A few days later, as the small plane took off, flying low over favorite secret coves, I closed my eyes to hold back the tears. It wasn't the tropical paradise with its white sand beaches and swaying palms that pulled at my heart. It was the gate and all the folks coming through it over the years, returning after a day at the beach.

Acknowledgments

With deep gratitude to:
La Finca's guests and managers for making
the dream come true

The people of Vieques, Puerto Rico, for
sharing that little piece of the world with us

Tom Payton and Steffanie Stevens at Trinity
for believing in the magic

Janice Shay for her editorial
wisdom & support

The whole duct-taped digital creative team
for help in manifesting the vision:
Lisa Fossen, Francesca Udeschini, Anne McGowan,
Katy McCoy, Tia Taylor, Daniel McCurdy, & Anika Colvin

Early editors & readers:
Amie Simon, Annie Brule, Elizabeth Cohen, Charlotte Adamson,
Celia Congdon, Juli Morser, & Wendy Poston

Additional photography:
Elliott Anderson, Kelly Thompson, & Andree Kehn

Additional art:
Alice Gardener, Evelyn Isaak,
Molly Isaak, & Nataly Knott

Permission for recipes, poems, & postcards:
Alice Waters, Coleman Barks, &
The Historic Archives, Fort Count Mirasol Vieques

Life support:
Del Webber

Corky Parker has had a diverse career as the creative director and cofounder of Merwin Creative, a film production company in Seattle; a small-scale sheep farmer; and owner of the eco-lodge La Finca Caribe, on Vieques Island, Puerto Rico. She is a graduate of Bennington College. Her work has been covered in the *New York Times*, *Wall Street Journal*, the *People's Daily*, the *Seattle Times*, *Outside*, *Gourmet*, *Adventure Travel*, and *Lonely Planet*. She lives in Port Townsend, Washington, and her website is at corkyparker.com.